odd ball knitting

odd ball knitting
creative ideas for leftover yarn

barbara albright

technical editing by jean lampe   photography by alexandra grablewski   illustrations by judy love

POTTER
CRAFT

New York

Copyright © 2005 by Barbara Albright

All rights reserved.

Published in the United States by
Potter Craft, an imprint of
the Crown Publishing Group, a division of
Random House, Inc., New York.
www.crownpublishing.com
www.clarksonpotter.com

POTTER CRAFT and CLARKSON N. POTTER
are trademarks and POTTER and colophon
are registered trademarks of Random
House, Inc.

Library of Congress Cataloging-in-
Publication Data
Albright, Barbara
Odd ball knitting: creative ideas for leftover
yarn / Barbara Albright; technical editing
by Jean Lampe; photography by Alexandra
Grablewski; illustrations by Judy Love.
   Includes index.
1. Knitting—Patterns   I. Lampe, Jean.
II. Title.
   TT825.A422   2004
   746.43'2041—dc22
2004019860

ISBN 1-4000-5351-X

Printed in China

Design by Jennifer Napier

10   9   8   7   6   5   4   3   2

First Edition

This book is dedicated to all my girlfriends from

- my childhood, when I first learned to knit (thanks, Mom!);
- those crazy college times;
- the days when we were young and single;
- the foodie world;
- my life as a mom in the audience, on the sidelines, and online;
- and, of course, to the artsy-craftsy fiber goddesses from every time in my life!

Acknowledgments

Many people need to be thanked for making this book possible. First, a huge, huge thank-you to Jean Lampe, the technical editor for this book. This is the third knitting book I have written with the guidance of Jean's eagle eyes. Her attention to detail as she makes sure these patterns are accurate is phenomenal. Jean loves everything about knitting and working with fibers, and she is a wealth of information. Each time I work on a book with her, I learn more and more.

Thanks to Roy Finamore for bringing me to Potter. Your encouraging e-mails about "Knit Thumbelina Knit" and "Keep Knittin' Kitten" brought a smile to my face when pattern writing loomed large. I am grateful to Jenny Frost for being a major-league publisher (and also a knitting fanatic) and for recognizing the need for this book. Thanks to my editor, Rosy Ngo, for pulling the pieces together and making this book happen. Thanks to Marysarah Quinn and Maggie Hinders, too. Photographer Alexandra (Alex) Grablewski took all the fabulous photographs in this book, making sure that readers would see each detail of the featured item. (Alex is also a knitter.) Thanks to her assistants, Jody Waldron and Todd Bonné, and makeup and hair artist Renée Majour, who made sure everyone looked fabulous! Thanks to the human models: Jessica Adams, Jivelle Calender, Max Gleason, Jack Rau Hinatsu, Betcee May, Jodi Murphy, Ashley Nylin, Ewa Zawol. And thanks to Ginger Rohr, the easygoing dog model, and her owners, Linda and Rick Rohr. Judy Love's illustrations clearly show how to accomplish the more challenging techniques.

Thanks to my husband, Ted Westray, and my children, Samantha and Stone, for surviving yet another book experience.

Thanks to my sister, Lynn Albright, and friends Victoria Downing, Beth Gunnell, Isabelle Vita Williams for pattern testing, and for the support of Marc Bailin, Rhonda Brown, and Janet and Roy Scanlon.

And special thanks to my own huge yarn stash, which is always ready, willing, and able to inspire, comfort, and enable me to dive into the next project.

Contents

introduction

Welcome!
We knit, therefore many of us have yarn—lots of it.

The goal of this book is to help you use this excess stash to create fabulous, fun, funky, and fashionable items. And perhaps it will even give you an excuse to go out and buy more yarn! The yarn section of each pattern includes guidelines so you can adapt the pattern to your own stash of yarns. Specific knitting instructions are provided that include the actual yarns used in each prototype. *However, do not limit yourself to the yarns used for the prototype designs, or you will never use your stash!* Throughout the book are Stash-Busting Tips. These tips will give you jumping-off points from which to do fabulous and creative things with your yarn.

Yarn and Fiber: It's a Way of Life

Some knitters organize their fiber by color and use a color wheel to plan how they will use the yarn. On the other hand, when colors are mixed together, there is a tendency to be more creative about combining colors. I once participated in a color class with Kaffe Fassett, expert colorist and designer. In the center of the room was a huge pile of balls, skeins, and strands of yarn in many colors. This chaotic collection of colors and textures excited the senses. It was easy to reach in and place the different yarns next to each other and test how they looked together.

In a later class, designer and book author Deborah Newton demonstrated that colors not usually to your liking can be turned into something great if you use them in a manner that pleases you. She asked us to knit swatches with yarn colors we wouldn't normally choose, and every time I happen upon the swatch I made, with its sparks of gaudy hot pink acrylic yarn, it makes me smile. It really does look okay! Grab a pair of knitting needles and challenge yourself by selecting your least favorite stash yarn color and try to figure out a way to make it look acceptable to you. By adding color, texture, or both, you might surprise yourself. The lesson is to keep an open mind about combining colors and texture from your stash to use for the designs in this book.

Part of the pleasure that comes from knitting is selecting yarns and color, whether at a store or from your stash. My good friend Marj Moureau calls this "playing with yarn." If you can't be knitting, the next-best thing is thinking about knitting. Sometimes the yarns tell you exactly what they want to be. For instance, a fluffy angora yarn might proclaim that it's perfect for a special collar treatment, or for trimming a hat brim, or

around the cuffs of gloves or mitts. If you bought the yarn for one project but later changed your mind, think about using it for something completely different.

Try not to overwork the design when using leftovers. Keep the design simple, and let the yarns do the work for you.

A quick way to decide if a particular combination of colors is pleasing is to wrap a piece of cardboard with varying amounts of each color. Study the colors, move them around, remove one or two colors, and add something else until you find the right combination for your project. By all means, use a color wheel and classic color theory if this helps you feel secure about selecting colors. (Books on color theory and color wheels are available at art supply stores.)

Inspiration Abounds!

Look around you. Wonderful color combinations exist in nature, clothing, quilts, artwork, museums, books, magazines, subway tiles, the peeling paint of an old barn—the possibilities go on and on. Think about color in terms of your own yarn stash. Designs created to use stash yarns often call for many colors in small amounts. Be ready to combine colors in ways you may not have done before. For help, look at your own collection of art, clothing, home décor, and garden flowers, and think what it is about their colors and textures that appeal to you. Perhaps you'll find that the very same colors in your favorite piece of artwork are also in your yarn stash. Most of us tend to gravitate to certain colorways and palettes, using them in the clothing we wear and the colors with which we decorate our homes.

Storing a Growing Stash

A few preparations should be made before storing yarns in order to protect your treasures and to help you locate suitable yarns when the perfect pattern comes along. I broadly classify my yarns by fiber content, storing cottons in one set of storage boxes, wool and other animal-based fibers in another. The designer yarns —or "wild stuff," as I like to call these specialty yarns—go in their own boxes. I also loosely categorize the yarns by weight, and I make a supreme effort to keep each yarn with its label. The label provides information about the number of yards, dye lots, the manufacturer or distributor's name, and care instructions. This information is invaluable, especially when combining yarns, because it will help determine if the yarns are compatible. Can they all be washed? Must some be dry-cleaned? Are some prone to shrinkage, while others are not? Will dye colors run? If you've knit a swatch with the yarn, label the swatch with the stitch pattern and needle size used; this information may be helpful someday. Large hangtags (available at office supply stores) are a good way to label these items.

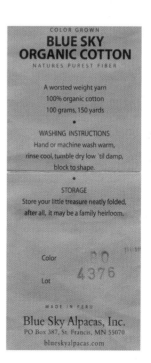

Keeping Critters Out

There is a four-letter word that instills fear in the hearts of most knitters: M-O-T-H! One of the best ways to avoid the heartbreak of moths' destroying your yarn or knitted items is to practice good housekeeping. Store clean yarns and knitted garments in a clean area. Clothes moths love dark, undisturbed environments. These cream-colored fiber-eaters are about ½ inch long and hide if disturbed. Don't confuse these moths with those seen flitting around lights.

Keep the yarn free from food, pet hair, and other debris that may provide food for the destructive moth larvae or attract other vermin. Inspect gifts of stash yarn before introducing it into your own precious stash. Check gift yarns carefully for signs of broken threads, which might indicate a moth infestation. Wash the yarn, winding it into a skein if necessary.

Some experts recommend freezing to eliminate pests. Yarn must be frozen for at least 48 to 72 hours at 0°F. At 10°F, pests can be eliminated, but you must freeze the yarn for a longer period. You can check your home freezer with a thermometer. A rule of thumb is that a freezer operating at 0°F will keep ice cream brick hard. This means that if your ice cream comes out of the freezer spoonable, the little buggers are alive and well, and there is no place they would rather warm up than in your precious stash.

To get rid of moths from yarn or a knitted item, place the yarn in a polyethylene bag, squeeze out the air, and tightly seal the bag. Freeze for two or three days, then remove the item to the refrigerator for a couple hours to thaw slowly, and then transfer to room temperature. Remove the yarn from the bag after it reaches room temperature. To make certain that all of the moths are destroyed, repeat the freezing process before removing the contents from the bag. Of course, you can turn to commercial moth repellents or a pest-control professional if things are really out of hand. In that case, it's probably wiser to discard the affected yarns.

A natural approach is to use dried herbs and other natural materials that are thought to help repel insects: cedar, eucalyptus, pennyroyal, lavender, and tansy. Tightly sealed cedar-lined closets and cedar chests can help prevent infestation, but after a few years, their volatile oils dry up, and they are no longer as effective.

Lavender Sachet

Lavender smells great and helps keep unwanted pests from turning your stash into their home.

Finished Size
Width: 4 inches (10 cm)
Length: 4 inches (10 cm)

Yarn
You will need about 37 yards (34 m) total of super fine yarn in Color A, using the same stitch pattern and gauge for the sachet. For the embroidery, you will need about 1 yard (91.5 cm) each of Colors B and C. Any yarn weight can be used.
We used Jager Farm Icelandic lace weight (hand-dyed, single-ply Icelandic wool; 290 yards [265 m]/2-ounce [57-g] skein):
Color A—Variegated Glass, 37 yards (34 m)
Color B—Variegated Purple, 1 yard (91.5 cm)
Color C—Grass, 1 yard (91.5 cm)

Needles
US size 0 (2 mm). *Adjust the needle size if necessary to obtain the correct gauge.*

Gauge
30 stitches and 76 rows = 4 inches (10 cm) in Pebble Stitch pattern

Notions
US size B-1 (2.25 mm) crochet hook; tapestry needle; about 8 inches (20 cm) x 4 inches (10 cm) of muslin (or any closely woven fabric) to make an inner pillow to hold the lavender; about 1.2 ounces (35 g) dried lavender (see Resources, page 121); sewing needle and thread to sew the muslin pillow together

Pattern Stitch

Pebble Stitch (even number of stitches)
Row 1: Knit.
Row 2: Purl.
Row 3: Knit 2 together (k2tog) across the row. (After completing this row, there will be half the number of sts on needle.)
Row 4: *Knit 1, work an open-style make 1 (M1) increase by inserting the right needle tip from front to back, under the running strand before the next st (this creates an untwisted loop over the needle), and knitting the loop without twisting it; repeat (rep) from * to end of row. At the end of the row, after the last st is worked, insert the left needle tip into the purl bump from the row below and knit it. (There is now the same number of sts cast on at the beginning.)
Rep these 4 rows for pattern.

Make the Sachet

Side 1: With Color A, cast on (CO) 30 sts. Knit in Pebble St for 7 repeats (28 rows). Beginning with a knit row, work 14 rows of stockinette stitch (St st). Work in Pebble St for 7 repeats. Bind off (BO).
Side 2: With Color A, cast on 30 sts. Knit in Pebble St until this side is the same length as Side 1. BO.

Finishing

Using Color B and a tapestry needle, embroider Lazy Daisies (see Techniques, page 116) on the St st band of Side 1, using the photograph as a guide. Using Color C, make a French knot (see Techniques, page 117) in each flower center.

Fold the muslin in half to form a 4-inch (10-cm) square. Leaving a 1-inch (2.5-cm) opening across the top, thread sewing needle with matching thread and sew 3 side edges together using a ¼-inch (6-mm) seam. Turn the muslin right-side out and fill with lavender. (A large funnel is helpful.) When the muslin pillow is filled, turn the ¼-inch (6-mm) seam allowance along the top opening to the wrong side and whipstitch (see Techniques, page 118) the opening together.

Place the knitted squares (Sides 1 and 2) over the muslin pillow. Pin around the edges to enclose the inner lavender-filled pillow.

Join both knitted pieces together as follows: With the crochet hook and Color A, work a row of single crochet (see Techniques, page 114) around all 4 sides of the sachet, and at the same time work 3 sc in each corner st to smoothly round the corners and prevent puckering. Keep your lavender sachet for yourself, or give it to someone special as a gift!

Yarns: Sizes and Substitutions

Yarns come in many weights and thicknesses, and manufacturers have given them a variety of names, making it confusing to tell just how fine or thick the yarn is. To add to the mix, terms may also vary by country.

However, when unsure if your yarns will work as a substitute for the yarn called for, *knit a swatch and check your gauge.* Does the gauge match? Does the fabric have the same hand? In other words, does it have the same drape, feel, and appearance? You might need a firm fabric for a bag, a more supple fabric for a scarf or sweater. For socks, a closely knit fabric will wear better. *Hellooooo!? Are you listening here? Make a swatch! (Go back and read this again. In fact, if necessary, read this paragraph before you start each project.)*

Ply refers to the number of strands that are twisted together, but this is not an indication of thickness or weight, as a thicker yarn may have fewer strands than a thinner one.

Other terms used to describe yarn are *smooth; soft-spun,* for those loosely spun; *novelty yarns,* for those that have an unusual ply style; *textured; thick-and-thin;* and *fleecy,* to name a few.

The Craft Yarn Council of America has developed standard definitions of yarn thickness. Knitting editors and members of the yarn industry worked diligently to come up with these categories.

Creating Your Own Yarn Style

As you search through your stash to find enough yarn for a project, don't forget that you can often use two or more strands of finer yarns held together as one to achieve the same gauge and body of a thicker yarn. Or, consider adding a row or two of wildly textured yarn for a unique effect. Try using a finer yarn for a couple of rows to create a lacy look. As always, make a swatch with your combinations to decide if you like its look and feel. If the yarn is washable, don't forget to wash the swatch. It's important to determine the final effect of your choices before you plunge headfirst into a large project.

6
super bulky

5
bulky

4
medium

3
light

2
fine

1
super fine

Craft Yarn Council of America's Standard Yarn Weight System

Yarn Weight Symbol & Category Names	1 SUPER FINE	2 FINE	3 LIGHT	4 MEDIUM	5 BULKY	6 SUPER BULKY
Other Names of Yarns in Category	Sock, Fingering, Baby	Sport, Baby	DK, Light Worsted, Four-ply, Jumper	Worsted, Afghan, Aran	Chunky, Craft, Rug	Bulky, Roving
Knit Gauge Range* in Stockinette Stitch to 4 inches (10 cm)	27–32 sts	23–26 sts	21–24 sts	16–20 sts	12–15 sts	6–11 sts
Recommended Needle in Metric Size Range	2.25–3.25 mm	3.25–3.75 mm	3.75–4.5 mm	4.5–5.5 mm	5.5–8 mm	8 mm and larger
Recommended Needle in U.S. Size Range	1 to 3	3 to 5	5 to 7	7 to 9	9 to 11	11 and larger

*GUIDELINES ONLY: The above reflect the most commonly used gauges and needle sizes for specific yarn categories.

How Much Yarn Do You Have?

The best way to figure out how much yarn you have is to read the label of the yarn. If the label is long gone and you can remember who made the yarn, check the manufacturer's Web site, where most current yarns are listed, or make a phone call to the distributor or your local yarn shop to find this information. Three Web sites that carry a wide variety of yarns are www.patternworks.com, www.personalthreads.com, and www.woodlandwoolworks.com. They may have the information for which you are looking.

By weighing the yarn and making basic calculations, you can figure out how many yards (meters) per ounce (gram) you have. An accurate digital postal scale is handy to have as part of your knitting equipment, as you can use it to weigh yarn precisely and easily. If you don't have a postal scale, the actual post office may weigh your skeins if you ask nicely and don't go at the busiest time. You can also ask your local supermarket if they will weigh your yarn on the digital scales in the deli section. (Wrap your skeins in plastic wrap so you don't get any fuzz on the scale!) Make friends with spinners, or look for a local spinning guild; they often have equipment for measuring and weighing yarns.

Basic Conversions

When You Know	Multiply By	To Find
inches	2.54	centimeters
yards	0.9144	meters
ounces	28.3495	grams
pounds (weight)	0.4535	kilograms

If you want to convert yards to meters or vice versa, and ounces to grams or vice versa, the following Web sites will do the computation for you: www.sciencemadesimple.com and www.benefitslink.com/cgi-bin/fiberlinkmanager/measurement_converter.cgi.

A chart for yardage of older yarns can be found at www.vintageknits.com/vintyarn1.html.

If you have mystery yarns with missing labels, try this site to help determine what type of fiber you have: www.lindrix.com/fabcontent.html.

How to Measure Your Yarn

The McMorran Yarn Balance is a delicate device that will help you figure out how many yards per pound there are in a specific yarn. This tool is available at many yarn stores and through craft catalogs, especially those that include spinning and weaving implements.

Cut a yarn strand long enough to drape over the balance arm of the McMorran Yarn Balance, and unbalance the arm so that it's pointing downward. The length to cut will vary depending upon the type of yarn. With a very fine yarn, such a length may be too long to drape over the arm without touching the counter, and thus must be folded in half once or twice in order for the yarn to hang over the balance arm unencumbered. To balance the arm, cut small amounts from the strand until the arm balances at midpoint. If you snip off too much yarn, add an extra piece or two until the arm balances. Then remove the yarn (and any extra pieces) from 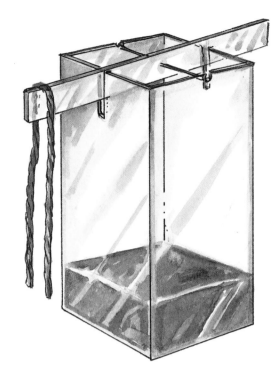 the balance arm, measure each piece, and add the measurements together. Now multiply the total by 100 to obtain the number of yards per pound. Then calculate the number of yards in your stash skein as follows:

- First, weigh the skein accurately. For this example, the skein weighs 1.75 ounces.
- Let's say the strand placed on the McMorran Yarn Balance measures 10 inches; 10 x 100 = 1,000 yards per pound (16 ounces).
- To calculate the yardage in 1 ounce, divide the 1,000 yards (computed by the McMorran scale) by 16 ounces = 62.5 yards per ounce.
- The 62.5 yards per ounce multiplied by 1.75 (the number of ounces in our skein) = 109.37 yards of yarn in the skein.
  A metric version of the McMorran scale is available.

One of the least expensive ways to determine yardage is simply to wind the yarn around something that has a measurable length—a chair back, for instance. Let's say your chair back has a 1-yard (1-m) circumference. Wind all the yarn around the chair back. Now count how many strands are wrapped around the chair. Multiply that number by the chair-back measurement. *Hint:* Always add an extra few inches or so to the calculated total to accommodate the buildup as yarn strands are wound on top of each other.

To save time, instead of winding large amounts of yarn around a chair back or similar object, you can weigh a smaller yarn length, and then multiply to calculate the yardage. (Have you noticed that a calculator is a good tool for stash owners?)

Here's an example:

- The skein weighs 3.5 ounces (99 g).
- Carefully measure 5 yards (4.5 m) by winding the yarn around the chair back. From these measurements, you determine that 5 yards weighs 0.38 ounces (10.77 g).
- Divide 3.5 (the number of ounces in the skein) by 0.38 (the weight of 5 yards) to determine how many 5-yard strands are contained within the 3.5-ounce skein. The answer is 9.2. Multiply 9.2 by 5 yards to obtain the length of the skein: approximately 46 yards (42 m).

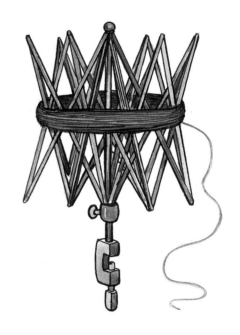

Yarn Swift—An umbrella-style yarn swift is another tool for measuring yarn. Set the swift spokes to a specific measurement, wind a piece of string around the center of the spokes once, and then measure the string to determine the measurement. Use string rather than yarn to determine the initial measurement because it's less likely to stretch, thus allowing for more accuracy. Adjust the swift until the string measures 1 yard (91.5 cm) so you'll know that each yarn wrap around the swift will be about 1 yard. Then wind the yarn around the same area. Count the number of yarn wraps to determine the yardage.

Niddy Noddy—An alternative tool, one frequently used by spinners, is a niddy noddy. The niddy noddy has a premeasured center stem with cross-arms at each end. Wind the yarn around the cross-arms from end to end. After winding, count the strands and multiply the total by the length of the center stem. Niddy noddies are commonly available in 18-inch (46-cm) and 1-yard (91.5-cm) lengths.

Just to Be Safe

When working with stash yarns and calculating the amount of yarn needed for a project, add at least 10 percent extra to the number of yards stated in a pattern. It's better to have a little extra yarn available than not enough, unless you're willing to take the gamble and live dangerously! Although the measuring methods suggested here are very good, they're not flawless. Remember, yarn stretches, and it's difficult to wind several skeins with uniform tension.

Can You Finish the Row?

Designs for stash yarns often use small amounts of many yarns or colors, and you may be left with just a few inches of yarn as the next row begins. Do you have enough yarn to finish the row, or should you join the next yarn? Some experts, including author, designer, and instructor Maggie Righetti, suggest that if the remaining yarn is 3 times the row width, that's enough to finish the row. Other experts calculate by stitches and gauge, allowing ¼ inch (6 mm) per stitch for fine yarn; ½ inch (1.3 cm) per stitch for lightweight yarn; ¾ inch (2 cm) per stitch for medium yarn; and 1 to 1½ inches (2.5–3.8 cm) per stitch for bulky yarns, plus a little extra to weave in the yarn tail. The book's technical editor, Jean Lampe, recommends that knitters consider the specific pattern stitch in their calculation, as a row with bobbles or ribbing will require more yarn to finish than a row of plain stockinette stitch. An alternative is to measure the yarn while making the gauge swatch. Work a row in pattern, mark the yarn at the beginning and end of the row, remove the stitches and measure the yarn (without stretching it). Then multiply the length by the number of stitches removed. Jot down the numbers on the pattern instructions for reference.

Are Your Yarns the Same Thickness?

To determine if two yarns are the same thickness, some fiber enthusiasts use the wraps per inch (WPI) method. The idea here is that if the yarns are the same thickness, they will provide the same gauge. To calculate the WPI, wrap the yarn around a ruler for 1 or more inches. Place each wrap next to the previous one without space between them, but do not allow the wraps to overlap. Continue the wraps for 1 or 2 inches, and then count them. Handle the yarn from the next skein the same way. Yarns that have the same WPI will work at the same gauge in the same pattern. The problem with this method is wrapping the yarns consistently and at the same tension.

When Too Much Is Indeed Too Much

Face it: You will *never* use some of your stash yarns. Why not have a stash party? Invite your knitting buddies over for a stash swap party. Promise wine and chocolate. Give guests an area where they can display their yarns—let the bartering and bargaining begin!

Don't Be Afraid to Give It Away

One knitter's trash is another knitter's treasure. Donate your excess yarn to charity, schools, or a scout troop. You might want to offer to teach knitting as well. Visit the charity section of www.interweave.com for a list of charitable organizations that may be able to use your extra yarn.

On the Receiving End

Learn to say no to people who want to give you yarn. If the yarn offered is wonderful, take it and enjoy. But if you're not sure you like it, and especially if the gift means you'll have to buy more yarn to use it, just say, *"No!"*

① for you and yours

Need a way to jazz up your wardrobe? Look no farther than your stash to meet your fashion needs. Because you already own the yarn, a stash project won't cost you a cent more. This chapter is full of designs you can knit for yourself, friends, and family.

Looking for a thoughtful gift for someone who needs a little support? An Amulet Pouch is just the thing to knit. To use up small amounts of glitzy yarns, why not make party purses? They are quick to knit, and the examples in this chapter have a fun loopy top. You can also knit a purse that's the perfect size for your personal stash of necessities, from lip gloss and a cell phone on up the scale.

If you have lots of yarn in your stash, try the I-80 Poncho. It's easy knitting as you go around and around, and at the end of your knitting, you have a stylish wearable security blanket of your own creation.

Amulet Pouch

All of us can use a little positive energy in our lives, and carrying around a symbol of luck might help. Who knows? One of these little amulet bags would make a great gift for someone you are concerned about. Add an angel, an acorn (for good luck and long life), or, as we've shown here, a piece of turquoise (the stone of happiness, health, and good fortune) to a hand-knit bag.

● ● ●

Stash-Busting Tip

Make someone a thoughtful little gift. Keep it small so you can present it to them soon. As you knit, you will probably find that you will be thinking of the recipient with every stitch you take, almost meditatively.

Finished Size
2½ inches (6.5 cm) x 2¼ inches (5.5 cm)

Yarn
You will need small yarn amounts ranging from 2 to 4 yards (1.8–3.6 m) in 5 colors. Or, use one variegated yarn throughout, plus a contrast color in round 8. Because the amulet pouch doesn't have to fit the measurements listed here, you have flexibility in the yarn weight and type.

We used LaLana Wools Forever Random Fines (handspun, sportweight, 60% Romney wool/40% yearling mohair; 118 yards [108 m]/2-ounce [57-g] skein):
Color A—Monet, about 3½ yards (3.2 m)
Color B—Yellow Brick Road, about 4 yards (3.6 m)

Phat Silk Fines (50% wool/50% bombyx silk; 98 yards [90 m]/2-ounce [57-g] skein):
Color C—Fustic Gold, about 2½ yards (2.3 m)

Dos Mujeres (2 ply, 55% mohair/45% merino wool; 122 yards [112 m]/2-ounce [57-g] skein):
Color D—Indigo Medium, about 2 yards (1.8 m)
Color E—Indigo Over Marigold, about 2½ yards (2.3 m)

Needles
US size 2 (2.75 mm) double-point (dpn), set of 4.
Adjust the needle size if necessary to obtain the correct gauge.

Gauge
11 stitches and 17 rounds = 2 inches (5 cm) in circular (circ) stockinette stitch (St st) (knit every round)

Notions
Tapestry needle; marker; small bead or button to use as a closure

Make the Pouch

With dpn and Color A, cast on (CO) 30 stitches (sts). Divide the sts onto 3 needles (10 sts on each needle) and join work into a circle, being careful not to twist the sts. Place a marker before the first CO st to identify the beginning of the round (rnd).

Rnds 1–2: With Color A, purl.

Rnd 3: Join Color B and knit.

Rnds 4–6 (3 rnds): With Color B, knit.

Rnd 7: Join Color C and knit.

Rnd 8: Using both Color C and D, *K2 in Color C, k1 in Color D*; repeat instructions between * * to the end of rnd.

Rnd 9: With Color C, knit.

Rnds 10–12 (3 rnds): Join Color E and knit.

Rnds 13–16 (4 rnds): Join Color B and knit.

Rnd 17: Join Color A and knit.

Rnds 18–19: With Color A, purl.

Rnd 20: Bind off (BO) all sts purlwise.

Cut a 12-inch (30.5-cm) strand of Color A. Thread tapestry needle and whipstitch (see Techniques, page 118) the bottom edges together. Cut 3 pieces of yarn, each about 40 inches (101.5 cm) long, using Colors C, D, and E. Leaving about ½-inch (1.3-cm) tails, knot the 3 strands together at one end and braid until about 1½ inches (3.8 cm) remain. Tie the ends into a knot, and trim the ends if necessary to ½ inch (1.3 cm).

Cut another 12-inch (30.5-cm) strand of Color A and thread tapestry needle. Attach the braided cord ends to each side of the bag. Using Color B, attach the bead to the front center of the bag as shown in the photograph.

Finishing

Thread tapestry needle with Color B.

On the back of bag, tie a knot in the end of thread and insert needle from wrong side (WS) to right side (RS) of work. Move over 1 st and insert needle from RS to WS of work, leaving a yarn loop long enough to enclose the bead or tiny button on the bag front. Knit with love and fill the bag with good energy.

Good-Luck Charms and Their Powers

The word *amulet* comes from the Arab word meaning "to carry," and it refers to an object that is carried on the body. In case you want to hedge your bets, here is a list of items and the properties with which they have historically been attributed:

Acorns—abundance and fertility

Bee—hard work, sweetness, wisdom, unselfishness

Beetle—as a scarab, symbolizes eternal life

Buttons—luck

Circle—eternity and wholeness; a circle surrounds good luck

Coins are lucky—especially those made in the year of your birth

Dove—peace, a messenger

Horseshoe—good luck and protection from evil spirits

Lapis—wear lapis, and you will always be loved

Stars—the symbol of angels

Turquoise—when worn around the neck, brings good luck

Wishbone—luck and marriage

Disco Purse

A whole sweater made with glitzy novelty yarns can be overwhelming, but when they are used prudently in a stylish bag, they can add an element of flair even to jeans and high heels. Quick to knit, the bags make great gifts. Next time you have a swatch you want to show off, think about turning it into a festive little purse. You can make the handle as long or short as you like—and perhaps you can use a double strand of beads.

Finished Size
Base width: 4½ inches (12 cm)
Width at top of bag: 7 inches (18 cm)
Height: 4½ inches (12 cm)

Yarn
You will need about 30 yards (28 m) of medium-weight yarn for Yarn A (the base yarn) and about 30 yards (28 m) of medium-weight yarn for Yarn B (the trim), using the same stitch pattern and gauge.

We used Berroco Quest (100% nylon; 82 yards [76 m]/1.75-ounce [50-g] skein):
Yarn A—#9808 Gold, 30 yards (28 m)

Trendsetter Yarns Dune (41% mohair, 30% acrylic, 12% viscose, 11% nylon, 6% metal; 90 yards [82 m]/1.75-ounce [50-g] skein):
Yarn B—#88 multicolor rust, navy, and plum, 30 yards (28 m)

Needles
US size 8 (5 mm) double-point (dpn), set of 4 or 5.
Adjust the needle size if necessary to obtain the correct gauge.

Gauge
20 stitches and 28 rounds = 4 inches (10 cm) in circular stockinette stitch (St st) (knit each round) with Yarn A
13 stitches = 4 inches (10 cm) in loopy stitch with Yarn B

Notions
Markers; tapestry needle; fabric and interfacing, about 8 inches x 10 inches (20.5 x 25.5 cm), to line the bag; sewing thread and sewing needle; 2 jewelry jumper rings; enough beads to string a 22-inch (58-cm) strap; 24 inches (61 cm) of flexible beading wire; 2 crimping beads; 1 large snap or magnetic closure

Note
Many novelty yarns are slippery, and knitters often find that wooden or plastic knitting needles hold the yarns better than metal needles.

Make the Purse

With dpn and Yarn A, cast on (CO) 44 stitches (sts). Join sts into a circle, being careful not to twist. Place a marker after the last st to identify the beginning of the round (rnd). Work in circular St st (knit every round) until the piece measures 3½ inches (9 cm) from the CO edge. Cut yarn, leaving 6-inch (15-cm) tail. Thread tapestry needle, weave tail to wrong side (WS) of work, and secure.

Join Yarn B and work in loopy stitch as follows:

Rnds 1 and 3: Purl.

Rnd 2: Knit.

Rnd 4: *K1, but don't allow the st to fall from the left needle. Bring the yarn forward (toward you) between the two needle tips and wrap the yarn clockwise around the left thumb, making a 1-inch (2.5-cm) loop (or longer, if you prefer). Take the yarn between the two needles to the back, then knit the same st (still on the left needle) through the back loop, k1*; repeat (rep) instructions between * * to end of rnd—(66 sts).

Rnd 5: *K2tog, k1*; rep instructions between * * to end of rnd—(44 sts).

Rnds 6 and 9: Purl.

Rnd 7: Rep Rnd 4.

Rnd 8: Rep Rnd 5.

Rnd 10: Knit.

Bind off (BO) all sts. Cut yarn, leaving 6-inch (15-cm) tail. Thread tapestry needle, weave tail to WS, and secure.

Cut a 12-inch (30.5-cm) strand of Yarn A. Thread tapestry needle and whipstitch (see Techniques, page 118) the bottom edges together.

Finishing

Using the bag as your guide, cut the lining fabric and interfacing to fit the inside of the bag, plus a ½-inch (1.5-cm) allowance on each side for the side seams, plus the same allowance to turn in to the WS around the top edge. Before seaming, each lining side should measure about 5½ inches (14 cm) wide at the bag base and gradually increase to 8 inches (20 cm) at the bag top. The total length is 10 inches (25.5 cm) before folding in half.

Holding lining pieces with right sides (RS) together, use threaded sewing needle to backstitch (see Techniques, page 118) the side seams together. Turn the lining so RS is facing outward; insert lining inside purse, with WS of lining and WS of purse together. Turn in about ½ inch (1.3 cm) lining seam allowance to WS around the top edge, and whipstitch (see Techniques, page 118) top of lining neatly to top of purse. Sew a jumper ring at each side seam, about ½ inch (1.3 cm) down from the top edge. String the beads on the wire, placing a crimping bead at each end. Loop one end of the wire through one ring. Turn and thread the wire back through the crimping bead and a few of the beads in the strap and crimp closed. Repeat on the other side. Sew the snap halves in the center near the top opening to close the bag. Turn bag to right side. Now go out and party!

Fiesta Bag

I was enchanted when I spied the red novelty yarn with streamers. However, like some other novelty yarns, when knit by itself this yarn was too scanty and did not make the dramatic impact it did in the ball. Combining the novelty yarn with a strand of multicolored cotton gives this bag its festive summery feeling.

Finished Size
Base width: 4¾ inches (12 cm)
Width of top of bag: 6 inches (15 cm)
Height: 4½ inches (12 cm)

Yarn
You will need about 72 yards (66 m) of medium-weight yarn for Yarn A (the base yarn) and about 10 yards (9 m) of novelty Yarn B (the trim), using the same stitch pattern and gauge.

We used Filatura Di Crosa Brilla (58% viscose, 42% cotton; 120 yards [110 m]/1.75-ounce [50-g] ball):
Yarn A—#9554 multicolor red, green, gold, about 72 yards (66 m)

Trendsetter Yarns Papi (100% polyamide; 71 yards [65 m]/.88-ounce [25-g] ball):
Yarn B—#23 Red, about 10 yards (9 m)

Needles
US size 3 (3.25 mm) double-point (dpn), set of 4 or 5.
Adjust the needle size if necessary to obtain the correct gauge.

Gauge
19 stitches and 27 rounds = 3 inches (8 cm) square in circular stockinette stitch (St st) (knit each round) with Yarn A. 20 stitches = 4 inches (10 cm) in loopy stitch with Yarns A and B held together as one

Notions
US size G/6 (4 mm) crochet hook; markers; tapestry needle; fabric and interfacing, about 7 x 10 inches (18 x 25.5 cm), to line the bag; sewing needle and sewing thread; 1 large snap or magnetic closure

Note
Many novelty yarns tend to be slippery. You might find that wooden or plastic knitting needles are easier to work with than metal needles.

Make the Bag

With dpn and Yarn A, cast on (CO) 60 stitches (sts). Join into a circle, being careful not to twist the sts. Place a marker after the last st to identify the beginning of the round (rnd). Work in St st until the piece measures 4 inches (10 cm) from the CO edge.

Top Edge
Rnd 1: With 1 strand each of Yarns A and B held together, purl all sts to end of rnd. If necessary, pull the streamers from Yarn B to the front.

Rnd 2: Knit with Yarn A only.

Rnd 3: With both yarns held together as one, *k1, but don't allow the st to fall from the left needle. Bring the yarn forward (toward you) between the two needle tips and wrap the yarn clockwise around the left thumb, making a 1-inch (2.5-cm) loop (or longer, if you prefer). Take the yarn between the two needles to the back, then knit the same st (still on the left needle) through the back loop, k1*; repeat (rep) instructions between * * to end of rnd.

Rnd 4: With Yarn A only, k2tog, k1; rep instructions between * * to end of rnd.

Rnd 5: Rep Rnd 3.

Rnd 6: Rep Rnd 4. Bind off (BO) all sts. Cut yarn, leaving 6-inch (15-cm) tail. Thread tapestry needle, weave tail to wrong side, and secure. Cut a 12-inch (30.5-cm) strand of Yarn A. Thread tapestry needle and whipstitch (see Techniques, page 118) the bottom edges together.

Finishing

Weave in loose ends. Using three 60-inch (152.5-cm) strands of Yarn A and the crochet hook, single crochet (see Techniques, page 114) a strap about 11 inches (28 cm) long. Cut yarn, leaving 4-inch (10-cm) tail. Insert tail through last loop on the hook and pull to tighten.

Sew each end of the crochet strap to the sides of the bag near the top edge. Cut the lining fabric and interfacing to fit the inside of the bag, allowing ½-inch (1.5-cm) side seams and the same allowance to turn in at the top edge. Before seaming, each lining side should measure about 5¾ inches (14.5 cm) wide at the bag base and gradually increase to 7 inches (18 cm) at the bag top. The total length is 10 inches (25.5 cm) before folding in half.

Sew the snap halves in the center of the opening, near the top edge, to close the bag. Now go out and party!!

Triple Triangle Extravaganza

Sometimes a skein of irresistible yarn begs to be purchased. However, once you get it home, then you think, "Now what?" This pattern is perfect for stash knitting because you can make the triangle as airy or dense as you want by adjusting the needle size.

Sizes (all triangles)
Kerchief: 18 inches wide x 12 inches long (46 x 30.5 cm)
I-cord ties: 39 inches (99 cm) from end to end

Small shawl: 52 inches wide x 25 inches long
(132 cm x 63.5 cm)

Medium shawl: 63 inches wide x 29 inches long
(160 x 73.5 cm)

Yarn
The kerchief requires about 95 yards (87 m).

The small shawl requires about 460 yards (420 m).

The medium shawl used about 518 yards (473 m) total. Some yarns were held together as one, and other yarns used as single strands. The following amounts were used:
- Yarns A and C—125 yards (114 m) each of solid-color mohair and multicolor silk-wool combination (one strand of each yarn held together and worked as one)
- Yarn B—155 yards (142 m) of multicolor mohair (used as single strand)
- Yarn D—70 yards (64 m) of alpaca (used as single strand)
- Yarn A—35 yards (32 m) of solid-color mohair (used as single strand)
- Yarn C—8 yards (7.3 m) of multicolored silk-wool (used as single strand)

For the kerchief, we used Classic Elite Yarn Premiere (50% pima cotton, 50% Tencel; 108 yards [99 m]/1.75-ounce [50-g] skein):
#5295 Eggplant, 95 yards (87 m)

For the small shawl, we used Blue Heron Yarns Rayon Seed (68% rayon seed, 32% cotton; 490 yard [448 m]/8-ounce [227-g] skein):
Old Gold, 460 yards (420 m)

For the medium shawl, we used a variety of Classic Elite yarns; some were single strands, and others were grouped together. LaGran Mohair (76.5% mohair, 17.5% wool, 6% nylon; 90 yards [82 m]/1.75-ounce [50-g] ball):
Yarn A—#6539 Eucalyptus Green, 160 yards (146 m)
Yarn B—#63502 April Evening, 155 yards (142 m)

Fame (85% rayon, 15% silk; 115 yd [105 m]/1.75-ounce [50-g] skein):
Yarn C—#1451 multicolor, 133 yards (122 m)

Inca Alpaca (100% alpaca; 109 yd [100 m]/1.75-ounce [50-g] skein):
Yarn D—#1142 Cajamaica Maroon, 70 yards (64 m)

Needles
Kerchief: US size 6 (4mm), 16 inches (40.5 cm);
US size 5 (3.75 mm) double-point needles (dpn), set of 2, for I-cord ties

Small shawl: US size 8 (5 mm), 24 inches (60 cm)

Medium shawl: US size 13 (9 mm), 47 inches (120 cm)
Use circular needles to accommodate stitch numbers.
Adjust the needle size if necessary to obtain the correct gauge.

Gauge
Kerchief: 19½ stitches and 40 rows = 4 inches (10 cm) in garter stitch

Small shawl: 16 stitches and 32 rows = 4 inches (10 cm) in garter stitch

Medium shawl: 9½ stitches and 20 rows = 4 inches (10 cm) in garter stitch

Notions
Tapestry needle

Notes
1. The basic design is a triangle that has a 3-stitch stockinette border on each side edge. The pattern is written to alternate a single-row lace pattern with a 4-row lace pattern. However, don't restrict yourself; insert the lace rows as desired and in the order of your choosing, as we have in these three pieces.

2. The ties on the kerchief need to be dense, so they should be knit at a tighter gauge. Use a US size 5 (3.75 mm) needle to make the I-cord.

Basic Pattern

Cast on (CO) 1 stitch (st).

Row 1: Wrong side (WS) knit 1 in front, back, then front loop again (k1f,b&f) to make 3 sts.

Row 2: Right side (RS) knit into the front and then the back loop of the same stitch (k1f&b), k1, k1f&b—(5 sts).

Row 3: Purl.

Row 4: K1f&b, k3, k1f&b—(7 sts).

Row 5: Purl.

Row 6: K2, k1f&b, k1f&b, k3—(9 sts).

Row 7: P3, k3, p3.

Row 8: K2, k1f&b, k2, k1f&b, k3—(11 sts).

Row 9: P3, k5, p3.

Row 10: K2, k1f&b, k4, k1f&b, k3—(13 sts).

Row 11: P3, k7, p3.

Row 12: K2, k1f&b, k6, k1f&b, k3—(15 sts).

Row 13: P3, k9, p3.

Row 14: K2, k1f&b, k8, k1f&b, k3—(17 sts).

Row 15: P3, k11, p3.

Row 16: K2, k1f&b, k10, k1f&b, k3—(19 sts).

Row 17: P3, k13, p3.

Row 18: K2, k1f&b, k12, k1f&b, k3—(21 sts).

Row 19: P3, k15, p3.

Row 20: K2, k1f&b, k14, k1f&b, k3—(23 sts).

Row 21: P3, k17, p3.

Row 22: K2, k1f&b, k16, k1f&b, k3—(25 sts).

Row 23: P3, k19, p3.

Row 24: *(Single-Row Lace Pattern)* K2, k1f&b, *yarn over (yo), knit 2 tog (k2tog); repeat (rep) from * across the row to last 4 sts, yo, k4—(27 sts).

Row 25: P3, k21, p3.

Row 26: K2, k1f&b, k20, k1f&b, k3—(29 sts).

Row 27: P3, k23, p3.

Row 28: K2, k1f&b, k22, k1f&b, k3—(31 sts).

Row 29: P3, k25, p3.

Row 30: K2, k1f&b, k24, k1f&b, k3—(33 sts).

Row 31: P3, k27, p3.

Row 32: K2, k1f&b, k26, k1f&b, k3—(35 sts).

Row 33: P3, k29, p3.

Row 34: K2, k1f&b, k28, k1f&b, k3—(37 sts).

Row 35: P3, k31, p3.

Row 36: K2, k1f&b, k30, k1f&b, k3—(39 sts).

Row 37: P3, k33, p3.

Row 38: K2, k1f&b, k32, k1f&b, k3—(41 sts).

Row 39: P3, k35, p3.

Row 40: K2, k1f&b, k34, k1f&b, k3—(43 sts).

Row 41: P3, k37, p3.

Row 42: K2, k1f&b, k36, k1f&b, k3 sts—(45 sts).

Row 43: P3, k39, p3.

Row 44: *(Four-Row Lace Pattern)* K2, k1f&b, *yo, k2tog; rep from * across the row to last 4 sts, yo, k4—(47 sts).

Row 45: P3, *yo, purl 2 together (p2tog); rep from * across the row to last 4 sts, ending with yo, p2tog, p2—(47 sts).

Row 46: K2, k1f&b, *yo, k2tog; rep from * across the row to last 4 sts, yo, k4—(49 sts).

Row 47: P3, *yo, p2tog; rep from * across row to last 4 sts, yo, p2tog, p2—(49 sts).

Row 48: K2, k1f&b, knit to last 4 sts, k1f&b, k3—(51 sts).

Row 49: P3, k45, p3—(51 sts).

Make the Kerchief

Rows 1–49: With larger-size circular (circ) needle, work same as Basic Pattern (Basic Patt)—(51 sts).

Rows 50–67 (18 rows): Repeat (rep) Rows 48 and 49 of Basic Patt, increasing (inc) 2 sts on each right side (RS) row as previously established in Basic Patt—(69 sts).

Row 68: Work Row 24 of Basic Patt—(73 sts).

Rows 69–84 (14 rows): Rep Rows 48 and 49 of Basic Patt—(87 sts).

Do not bind off (BO). Leave sts on needle. Cut yarn, leaving 4-inch (10-cm) tail.

Finishing

I-Cord Ties and Edging
This cord is worked continuously from the end of one tie, across the top of the kerchief, and then on to form the second tie (see I-cord tie illusration).

First I-Cord Tie
Change to smaller-size dpn, join yarn, and CO 4 sts. *Without turning the needle, slide the sts to other end of the needle. The working yarn will be at the other end of the needle. Pull the yarn across the back of the work and toward the front of the needle, and knit the sts as usual; rep from * until the I-cord tie measures 10 inches (25.5 cm). Do not bind off.

Attach the I-cord to the 87 live kerchief sts on the main needle as follows: *k3 I-cord sts, k2tog (this will be one I-cord st and one live st from the kerchief); slide sts to other end

of smaller circ needle, same as when making I-cord tie; rep from * until all live kerchief sts have been attached to the I-cord and four I-cord sts remain on the smaller circ needle. Do not BO.

Second Tie
Work the four-st I-cord for another 10 inches (25.5 cm), same as the first tie. Cut yarn, thread tail through tapestry needle, and insert needle through the center of the I-cord sts. Weave in loose ends to wrong side (WS) of work.

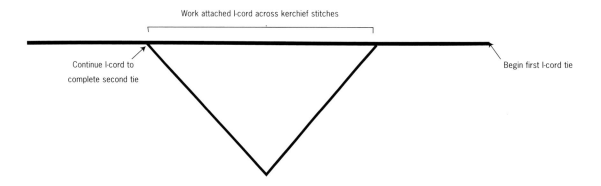

Work attached I-cord across kerchief stitches

Continue I-cord to complete second tie

Begin first I-cord tie

Make the Small Shawl

Rows 1–23: With yarn and circ needle, CO 1 st, and work first 23 rows of Basic Pattern (Basic Patt)—(25 sts).

Row 24: Work Single-Row Lace Pattern—(27 sts).

Rows 25–43 (19 rows): Work same as in Basic Patt—(45 sts).

Rows 44–47 (4 rows): Work Four-Row Lace Pattern—(49 sts).

Rows 48 and 49: Work same as in Basic Patt—(51 sts).

Rep Rows 48–49 same as in Basic Patt from this point on, working 2 more sts between increases on even-numbered rows as established, and inserting the single-row and 4-row lace patts as directed.

Rows 50–67 (18 rows): Rep Rows 48–49 of Basic Patt—(69 sts).

Row 68: Rep Row 24 of Basic Patt—(71 sts).

Rows 69–87 (19 rows): Work Rows 48–49 of Basic Patt—(89 sts).

Rows 88–91 (4 rows): Rep Rows 44–47 of Basic Patt—(93 sts).

Rows 92–113 (22 rows): Work Rows 48–49 of Basic Patt—(115 sts).

Row 114: Rep Row 24 of Basic Patt—(117 sts).

Rows 115–133 (19 rows): Rep Rows 48–49 of Basic Patt—(135 sts).

Rows 134–137 (4 rows): Rep Rows 44–47 of Basic Patt—(139 sts).

Rows 138–157 (20 rows): Rep Rows 48–49 of Basic Patt—(159 sts).

Row 158: Rep Row 24 of Basic Patt—(161).

Rows 159–177 (20 rows): Rep Rows 48–49 of Basic Patt—(179 sts).

Rows 178–181 (4 rows): Rep Rows 44–47 of Basic Patt—(183 sts).

Rows 182–185 (4 rows): Rep Rows 48–49 of Basic Patt—(187 sts).

Row 186: Bind off all stitches using decrease bind-off method (see Techniques, page 119). Cut yarn, leaving 4-inch (10-cm) tail. Insert tail through last stitch and pull to tighten. With tapestry needle, weave in all loose ends on WS of work and secure.

Make the Medium Shawl

Rows 1–23: With 1 strand each of Yarns A and C held together as one, CO 1 st and work Rows 1–23 of Basic Pattern (Basic Patt)—(25 sts).

Row 24: (*Single-Row Lace Pattern*) With A and C, k2, k1f&b, *yarn over (yo), knit 2 together (k2tog); repeat (rep) from * across the row to last 4 sts, yo, k4—(27 sts).

Rows 25–29 (5 rows): With A and C, work same as Basic Patt—(31 sts). Cut yarns, leaving 4-inch (10-cm) tails.

Rows 30–35 (6 rows): Join single strand of Yarn B and continue same as Basic Patt—(37 sts). Cut yarn, leaving 4-inch (10-cm) tail.

Rows 36–39 (4 rows): Join single strand of Yarn C, continue same as Basic Patt—(41 sts).

Rows 40–43 (4 rows): With A and C held together as one, continue same as Basic Patt—(45 sts).

Rows 44–47 (4 rows): With A and C, work Four-Row Lace Pattern same as Basic Patt—(49 sts). Cut yarn, leaving 4-inch (10-cm) tail.

Rows 48–49 (2 rows): Join B, continue same as Basic Patt—(51 sts).

Rows 50–55 (6 rows): With B, rep Rows 48–49 same as Basic Patt—(57 sts). Cut yarn, leaving 4-inch (10-cm) tail.

Rows 56–63 (8 rows): Join D, repeat Rows 48–49 same as Basic Patt—(65 sts). Cut yarn, leaving 4-inch (10-cm) tail.

Rows 64–69 (6 rows): Join B, rep Rows 48–49 same as Basic Patt—(71 sts).

Rows 70–73 (4 rows): With B, rep Rows 44–47 same as Basic Patt—(75 sts).

Rows 74–77 (4 rows): With B, rep Rows 48–49 same as Basic Patt—(79 sts). Cut yarn, leaving 4-inch (10-cm) tail.

Rows 78–89 (12 rows): Join A and C, rep Rows 48–49 same as Basic Patt—(93 sts). Cut yarn, leaving 4-inch (10-cm) tail.

Rows 90–97 (8 rows): Join D, rep Rows 48–49 same as Basic Patt —(99 sts).

Rows 98–101 (4 rows): With D, rep Rows 44–47 same as Basic Patt—(103 sts). Cut yarn, leaving 4-inch (10-cm) tail.

Rows 102–111 (10 rows): Join B, rep Rows 48–49 same as Basic Patt —(113 sts). Cut yarn, leaving 4-inch (10-cm) tail.

Rows 112–121 (10 rows): Join A and C, rep Rows 48–49 same as Basic Patt—(123 sts).

Rows 122–125 (4 rows): With A and C, rep Rows 44–47 same as Basic Patt—(127 sts).

Rows 126–129 (4 rows): With A and C, rep Rows 48–49 same as Basic Patt—(131 sts). Cut yarn, leaving 4-inch (10-cm) tail.

Rows 130–139 (10 rows): Join B, rep Rows 48–49 same as Basic Patt—(141 sts).

Row 140: With B, BO all sts using the decrease bind-off method (see Techniques, page 119).

Finishing

Cut yarn, leaving 4-inch (10-cm) tail. Insert tail through last stitch and pull to tighten. With tapestry needle, weave in all loose ends on WS of work and secure.

● ● ●

Stash-Busting Tip

Think outside the box and think triangularly! Because each design featured here begins at its lower tip with just one stitch, then gradually increases to the desired width, you can just keep knitting until you run out of yarn.

Diagonal Scarves

I love ribbon yarns and have several irresistible skeins in my stash. Because ribbon yarn tends to create a very clingy fabric, a scarf is an excellent choice. Find your most exciting skeins and try this easy diagonal scarf pattern worked on large-size needles. The scarf includes rows of eyelets, which work up fast and take very little yarn. The glorious luminescent yarn used in this project is enhanced by the addition of beads and charms, making a scarf that appears almost as wonderful as a hand-crafted necklace. By simply changing the needle size, this basic concept was used to make a second version in beautiful multicolored mohair. You can adapt this pattern to the yarns in your stash. Layer these scarves and wear them together for a particularly dramatic and textural look.

Stash-Busting Tip

Think diagonally. Even a basic garter stitch scarf is interesting to knit when worked on the diagonal. Make a long and wide diagonal rectangle for a bench cushion or a shawl. A diagonal square would make a good chair cushion or a pillow top.

Finished Sizes
Ribbon Scarf: Width: 6 inches (15 cm)
Length: 45 inches (114 cm)

Mohair Scarf: Width: 8 inches (20 cm)
Length: 45 inches (114 cm)

Yarn
You will need about 158 yards (144 m) total of ribbon yarn, using the same pattern stitch and gauge.

The mohair scarf requires about 200 yards (183 m) total of fine kid mohair, using the same pattern stitch and gauge.

For the Ribbon Scarf, we used Colinette Giotto (50% cotton, 40% rayon, 10% nylon; 158 yards [144 m]/3.5-ounce [100-g] skein): #93 Lapis, about 158 yards (144 m)

For the Mohair Scarf, we used Color Me Illusions (100% kid mohair; 500 yards [457 m]/3.5-ounce [100-g] skein): Regal, handpainted, about 200 yards (183 m)

Needles
Ribbon Scarf: US size 15 (10 mm)

Mohair Scarf: US size 11 (8 mm)
Adjust the needle size if necessary to obtain the correct gauge.

Gauge
Ribbon Scarf: 20 stitches and 22 rows = 6 inches (15 cm) in pattern on size 15 (10 mm) needles

Mohair Scarf: 15 stitches and 16 rows = 4 inches (10 cm) in pattern on size 11 (8 mm) needles

Notions
US size H (5 mm) crochet hook; tapestry needle; 40 to 50 glass beads and/or charms; color-coordinated sewing thread to match the scarf; sewing needle to sew beads into the scarf; Big Eye needle (see Resources, page 123) to thread the beads onto the mohair fringe.

Note
If adding fringe to your scarf, cut the fringe strands before beginning to knit.

Make the Ribbon Scarf

Scarf Point, Increase Rows
Cast on (CO) 1 stitch (st).

Row 1: Increase (inc) 2 sts by knitting into the front loop, then the back loop, and then the front loop of the st (k1f,b&f)—(3 sts).

Row 2: Slip (sl) 1 st purlwise (pwise), inc 1 st by knitting into the front then back loop of the next st (k1f&b), knit the remaining sts—(4 sts).

Row 3: Sl 1 pwise, k1f&b in next st, knit to end of row—(5 sts).

Row 4: Sl 1 pwise, k1f&b in next st, knit to end of row—(6 sts).

Rows 5–13 (9 rows): Repeat (rep) Row 4—(15 sts).

Row 14: (*Increasing Lace Row*, worked only in the point of the scarf) Sl 1 pwise, k1f&b, *yarn over (yo), knit 2 sts together (k2tog)*; rep instructions between * * to last 3 sts, end row with k2tog, k1—(16 sts).

Rows 15–18 (4 rows): Rep Row 4—(20 sts).

Main Body—Diagonal Pattern

Row 19: (*Shaping Row*) Sl 1 pwise, k1f&b, knit to last 3 sts, k2tog, k1.

Row 20: Sl 1 pwise, knit to end of row.

Rows 21–29 (9 rows): Rep Rows 19 and 20, finishing with a Row 19.

Row 30: (*YO Lace Row*) Sl 1 pwise, *yo, k2tog;* rep instructions between * * across the row to the last 3 sts, end row with k2tog, k1.

Continue working Rows 21 through 30 until the scarf measures about 39 inches (99 cm) or desired length. End having completed a Row 30 (*YO Lace Row*).

Scarf Point, Decrease Rows

Rows 1–19: Sl 1 pwise, k2tog, knit to end of row (after Row 19 is finished, 1 st remains). Cut yarn, leaving 4-inch (10-cm) tail. Insert tail through last stitch on needle and pull to tighten. See Finishing below.

Make the Mohair Scarf

Work same as for Ribbon Scarf through Row 14 (*Increasing Lace Row*)—(16 sts).

Rows 15–25 (11 rows): Sl 1 pwise, k1f&b, knit to end of row —(27 sts).

Row 26: Rep Row 14 (*Increasing Lace Row*)—see Ribbon Scarf—(28 sts).

Rows 27–28 (2 rows): Rep Row 15—(30 sts).

Main Body—Diagonal Pattern

Work the Main Body—Diagonal Pattern same as for Ribbon Scarf (Rows 21–30) until scarf measures about 39 inches (99 cm) or desired length. End having completed a Row 30 (*YO Lace Row*).

Scarf Point, Decrease Rows

Repeat Row 1 of Scarf Point Decrease Rows (see Ribbon Scarf instructions) until 18 sts remain. Work a lace row on the next row as follows: Sl 1, *k2tog, yo*; rep instructions between * * to last 3 sts, end row with k2tog, k1.

Resume working Row 1 of Scarf Point Decrease Rows until 1 st remains. Cut yarn, leaving 4-inch (10-cm) tail. Insert the tail through the last st on the needle and pull to tighten.

Finishing

With a tapestry needle, weave in loose yarn tails along the side edges and secure.

Fringe for Mohair Scarf
(optional)

Wind yarn around a 6-inch (15-cm) length of cardboard. Cut the yarn at one end. Make sixty 12-inch (31-cm) strands. **To make the fringe,** *holding two strands of yarn together side by side, fold the strands in half to form a loop at one end. Working from front to back, insert the crochet hook into the first stitch on one end of the scarf. (For a sturdier edge, insert the hook so that three strands of edge yarns are included in the border.) Catch the folded loops and pull through the work. Bring the cut ends through the folded loops and tighten*; rep instructions between * * until each st on the narrow end of the scarf has a fringe strand attached. Repeat fringe process on the other end of the scarf.

To decorate the scarf with beads and charms, thread a few of the beads onto the yarn fringe strands, dispersing them evenly across the fringe. Sew the beads in place, or tie a double overhand knot under each bead to hold in place. Arrange the remaining beads on the bottom 6 inches (15 cm) of each end of scarf and sew into place with the needle and thread. Go out and dazzle the world!

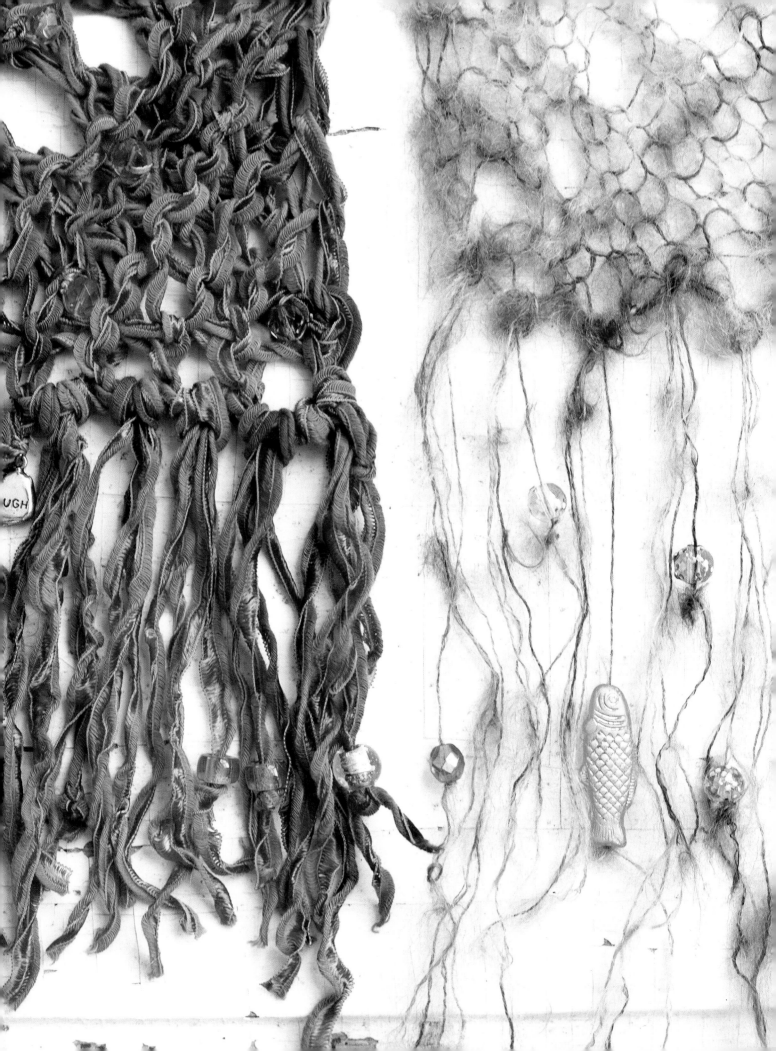

Ted's Scarf

This scarf is knitted using a diagonal pattern that looks attractive on both sides. Using the appropriate yarns from your stash, make the stripes wider, smaller, or change the colors. You can also make a narrower, lighter-weight scarf by using finer yarns, smaller-size needles, and the same stitch pattern.

Finished Size
Width: 11 inches (28 cm)
Length: 77 inches (195.5 cm)

Yarn
You will need about 680 yards (622 m) total of medium-weight yarn; approximately 55 yards (50 m) for each of 12 colors, using the same stitch pattern and gauge.

We used Mission Falls 1824 Wool (100% merino superwash; 85 yards [78 m]/1.75-ounce [50-g] skein), about 55 yards (50 m) each of the following colors:
Color A—#22 Ink
Color B—#18 Spruce
Color C—#26 Zinnia
Color D—#28 Pistachio
Color E—#24 Damson

Color F—#9 Nectar
Color G—#27 Macaw
Color H—#11 Poppy
Color I—#17 Heath
Color J—#2 Stone
Color K—#30 Teal
Color L—#21 Denim

Needles
US size 8 (5 mm). *Adjust the needle size if necessary to obtain the correct gauge.*

Gauge
19 stitches and 26 rows = 4 inches (10 cm) in pattern stitch

Notions
Tapestry needle

Pattern Stitches

Seed Stitch (worked over even number of stitches)
Row 1: *K1, p1; repeat (rep) from * across row.

Row 2: *P1, k1; rep from * across row.

Rep these 2 rows for pattern (patt).

Main Pattern Stitch (multiple of 8 sts plus 6)
Row 1: P3, *k5, p3; rep from * to last 3 sts, k3.

Row 2: P4, *k3, p5; rep from * to last 2 sts, k2.

Row 3: P1, k5, *p3, k5: rep from * to end of row.

Row 4: K1, p5, *k3, p5; rep from * to end of row.

Row 5: K4, *p3, k5; rep from * to last 2 sts, p2.

Row 6: K3, *p5, k3; rep from * to last 3 sts, p3.

Row 7: K2, p3, *k5, p3; rep from * to last st, k1.

Row 8: P2, k3, *p5, k3; rep from * to last st, p1.

Rep the above 8 rows for patt.

Make the Scarf

With Color A, cast on (CO) 52 sts.

Border: Knit 3 rows in Seed Stitch (st). Begin working in random-size stripes as follows: **With A,** work 3 sts in established Seed St patt for the first side edge border, then starting with Row 1 of Main Patt, work 46 sts in the Main Patt, then finish row with the last 3 sts in established Seed St patt for the second side edge border.

Continue working 3 sts as Seed St side borders at the beginning and end of each row, and the Main Patt worked over 46 sts between the side borders. Cut or break Color A after completing 36 rows in Main Patt, leaving a 4-inch (10-cm) yarn tail to weave in later. Work even in established patterns, changing colors as follows:

With B, work 6 rows.

With C, work 16 rows.

With D, work 10 rows.

With E, work 12 rows.

With F, work 6 rows.

With G, work 10 rows.

With H, work 20 rows.

With I, work 10 rows.

With J, work 14 rows.

With K, work 20 rows.

With D, work 10 rows.

With A, work 8 rows.

With F, work 14 rows.

With G, work 6 rows.

With E, work 22 rows.

With C, work 10 rows.

With B, work 8 rows.

With J, work 14 rows.

With I, work 16 rows.

With F, work 10 rows.

With H, work 16 rows.

With D, work 6 rows.

With G, work 12 rows.

With E, work 10 rows.

With C, work 16 rows.

With J, work 16 rows.

With K, work 12 rows.

With F, work 10 rows.

With I, work 18 rows.

With D, work 22 rows.

With H, work 10 rows.

With B, work 22 rows.

With C, work 6 rows.

With L, work 40 rows.

Border: With L, knit 3 rows of Seed St.

Finishing

Bind off (BO) all stitches. With tapestry needle, weave in loose yarn tails along the side edges (see Techniques, page 119) and secure.

I-80 Poncho

While this poncho takes a lot of knitting, it's a fun project to knit on a road trip and requires very little fitting and sewing. For the poncho shown, I used wide bands of color, but using more colors and making narrower stripes will also work well. Make this poncho as long and as dramatic as you would like, or keep it short to make a capelet.

Finished Size
Circumference, lower edge: 176 inches (4.51 m)
Length: About 35 inches (89 cm) from neck to lower edge. The poncho is worked from the neck down, so the length is easily adjusted depending on the amount of yarn you have.

Yarn
You will need about 450 yards (412 m) of medium-weight yarn in main color and about 1433 yards (1310 m) total in contrast colors, using the same stitch pattern and gauge.

We used Classic Elite Montera (50% llama, 50% wool; 127 yards [116 m]/3.5-ounce [100-g]) skein:
Color A—#3840 Tuscan Hills, 450 yards (412 m)
Color B—#3885 Bolsita Orange, 350 yards (320 m)
Color C—#3832 Puma Magenta, 50 yards (46 m)
Color D—#3853 Black Cherry, 120 yards (110 m)
Color E—#3881 Lima Green, 254 yards (232 m)
Color F—#3852 Peruvian Potato, 65 yards (59 m)
Color G—#3825 Kansas Sunflower, 51 yards (47 m)
Color H—#3868 Ancient Orange, 270 yards (247 m)
Color I—#3887 Pear, 273 yards (250 m)

Needles
US size 6 (4 mm), 16 inches (40.5 cm) and 29 inches (73.5 cm) circular (circ); US size 8 (5 mm) circ in several lengths. Use several circ needles in various lengths to accommodate the number of stitches (use these needles as if they were double-point needles). *Adjust the needle size if necessary to obtain the correct gauge.*

Gauge
17 stitches and 25 rounds = 4 inches (10 cm) in circular stockinette stitch (St st) on larger-size needles

Notions
Markers, with one marker in a different color from the others; tapestry needle

Notes
1. When casting on, place a marker after every 25 stitches (sts) to make it easier to count the stitches.

2. The ruffled edge around the neck is knit back and forth until the decreases (dec) are finished, then joined into a circle and knit in rounds (rnds).

3. The ruffle around the lower edge is created by working one side at a time so the work is more manageable. After completing each section, stitch the short ruffle edges together with mattress st (see Techniques, page 118).

4. Make 1 (m1) (see Abbreviations, page 120).

Make the Poncho

Ruffled Neck
Using smaller-size circ needle in one or more 29-inch lengths (or whatever length comfortably holds the stitches) and Color A, cast on (CO) 367 sts.

Row 1: *Knit 2 together (k2tog), yarn over (yo)*; repeat (rep) instructions between * * across the row, ending yo, k1—(368 sts).

Row 2: Purl.

Row 3: K2tog across the row—(184 sts).

Row 4: Purl.

Row 5: K2tog across the row—(92 sts).

Row 6: Purl row onto 16-inch needle.

Place marker to mark the beginning of the rnd and join work into a circle, being careful not to twist the sts. Work in rounds (rnds) of k1, p1 ribbing until the neck measures 4½ inches (11.5 cm) from beginning of ribbing, placing 3 additional markers each with 23 sts between them. Use different markers or colors from the first marker used to identify the rnd beginning so you can easily identify the beginning of each rnd.

Poncho Body
Switch to larger-size needles.

Rnd 1: Slip (sl) marker, make 1 (m1), * knit until 1 st before the next marker, m1, k1, sl marker, m1; rep from * 2 more times, knit to 1 st before end of rnd, m1, k1—(100 sts).

Rnd 2: Knit.

Rep Rnds 1 and 2, following the color sequence below:

Color A—Work 8 rnds (includes Rnds 1 and 2 worked above)—(132 sts).

Color B—Knit 1 rnd—(140 sts).
Purl 1 rnd.

Color A—Knit 2 rnds—(148 sts).

Color C—Knit 1 rnd—(156 sts).
Purl 1 rnd.

Color A—Knit 2 rnds—(164 sts).

Color D—Knit 1 rnd—(172 sts).
Purl 1 rnd.

Color E—Knit 2 rnds—(180 sts).

Color F—Knit 1 rnd—(188 sts).
Purl 1 rnd.

Color E—Knit 2 rnds—(196 sts).

Color G—Knit 1 rnd—(204 sts).
Purl 1 rnd.

Color E—Knit 2 rnds—(212 sts).

Color H—Knit 1 rnd—(220 sts).
Purl 1 rnd.

Color I—Knit 2 rnds—(228 sts).

Color C—Knit 1 rnd—(236 sts).
Purl 1 rnd.

Color I—Knit 2 rnds—(244 sts).

Color F—Knit 1 rnd—(252 sts).
Purl 1 rnd.

Color I—Knit 6 rnds—(276 sts).

Color B—Knit 14 rnds—(332 sts).

Color E—Knit 12 rnds—(380 sts).

Color D—Knit 8 rnds—(444 sts).

Color A—Knit 14 rnds—(500 sts).

Color H—Knit 14 rnds—(556 sts).

Color I—Knit 12 rnds—(604 sts).

Color B—Knit 14 rnds—(660 sts).

Color E—Knit 4 rnds—(676 sts).

Color C—Knit 1 rnd—(684 sts).
Purl 1 rnd.

Color E—Knit 2 rnds—(692 sts).

Color D—Knit 1 rnd—(700 sts).
Purl 1 rnd.

Color E—Knit 2 rnds—(708 sts).

Color G—Knit 1 rnd—(716 sts).
Purl 1 rnd.

Color A—Knit 2 rnds—(724 sts).

Color F—Knit 1 rnd—(732 sts).
Purl 1 rnd.

Color A—Knit 2 rnds—(740 sts).

Color H—Knit 1 rnd—748 sts).
Purl 1 rnd.

Ruffle

With A, working in rows, back and forth, in St st, work ¼ section (one side) of lower edge at a time—(187 sts).

Row 1: Knit into the front and then the back loop of the same stitch (k1f&b) in every st to end of section—(374 sts).

Row 2: Purl.

Row 3: K1f&b in every st to end of row—(748 sts).

Row 4: Purl.

Row 5: *K2tog, yo*; rep instructions between * * to end of row. Bind off (BO) all sts. Rep from Row 1 for each of the remaining 3 sections.

Finishing

With a tapestry needle threaded with Color A, sew together the neck ruffle seams and join the ruffles around the base of the poncho with mattress st (see Techniques, page 118). With a tapestry needle, weave in loose yarn tails to wrong side (WS) of work and secure.

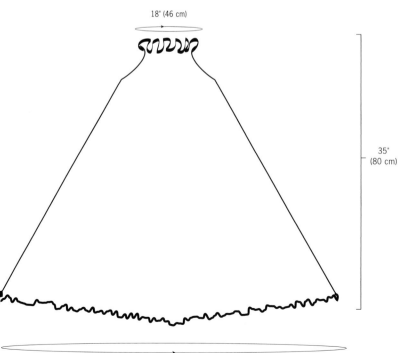

18" (46 cm)

35" (80 cm)

176" (454.5 cm)

Make Your Own Beaded Stitch Markers

Stitch markers help you identify specific places or patterns within your work. A marker also shows the progress made in your knitting, which should put a smile on your face, particularly if you use a festive marker like the beaded ones shown here.

To make the markers, you will need:

- Wire cutters

- 24-gauge wire

- Size 11 (8.0 mm) knitting needle or 8.0 mm crochet hook

- Beads with holes large enough to slip over 2 strands of the wire held together

- Round-nose pliers

With wire cutters, cut a 3-inch (7.5-cm) piece of wire. Fold it in half around the knitting needle or the thick end of the crochet hook and smoothly and tightly twist the two ends around each other. Slide the desired number of beads onto the wires. Using the round-nose pliers, twist the wires in a curlicue fashion to hold the beads in place. Rub your fingertips over the end to make sure there are no exposed rough ends that might snag the knitting. If necessary, use the pliers to press and flatten the top of the coils.

2

for heads and toes

When we're wearing hand-knitted headwear or footwear, the world just seems a better place. Hats, headbands, and socks don't take much yarn and are usually quick to make. For instance, the Easy Rolled-Edge Hat (page 55) is made with bulky yarn or with several strands of thinner yarn held together as one yarn. If you need a quick gift for someone, here's a hat you can put together in a few hours.

Use the knitted flowers on the San Francisco Headbands (page 50) to trim other items such as handbags, skirts, sweaters, and scarves. Headbands and fanciful knitted flowers are a great way to use bits and pieces of novelty yarns.

Don't neglect the top of your socks, either! Specialty yarns and beads can form a fabulous top edge to jazz up any pair of socks. Check out the Walk on the Wild Side Slipper Socks and the more subdued striped version (page 57).

Both skullcaps in this chapter are knit with fine yarn but could incorporate many colors from your stash. Think about adding interesting toppers to hats. The beaded tassel on the Striped Skullcap was inspired by Johnny Depp's pirate wear in the movie *Pirates of the Caribbean*. (Movie and live theater costumes are great sources for design and color ideas.)

San Francisco Headbands

A sturdy, smooth yarn was used along with a strand of fluffy, glitzy yarn to make these two headbands. The sample headbands shown here fit average head sizes. To make other sizes, simply cast on more or fewer stitches in multiples of 4. (See the head measurement guidelines, page 53.)

Finished Size
The headbands should fit snugly so they stay in place.

Version #1 (green and orange band with orange flower)
Width: 3½ inches (9 cm)
Circumference: 15 inches (38 cm)

Version #2 (fuzzy bouclé band in a combination of reds, blues, green, and purple, with red-trimmed yellow flower)
Width: 4 inches (10 cm)
Circumference: 16 inches (40.5 cm)

Yarn
You will need about 45 yards (42 m) of each yarn to create the headband, and about 8 to 10 yards (7 to 9 m) to make each flower.

For Version #1, we used Classic Elite Montera (50% Llama/50% Wool; 127 yards [116 m]/3.5-ounce [100-g] skein):
#3887 Pear, about 48 yards (44 m), for the headband and flower center embroidery
#3885 Bolsita Orange, about 8–10 yards (7–9 m), for the flower

Crystal Palace Fizz (100% polyester; 120 yards [110 m]/1.75-ounce [50-g] skein)
#7129 multicolor, a combination green, orange, red, about 45 yards (42 mm), for the headband

For Version #2, we used Dalegarn Sisik (30% wool, 30% mohair, 34% acrylic, 6% viscose; 148 yards [136 m]/1.75-ounce [50-g] ball):
#167 red, about 45 yards (42 m) for headband and flower embroidery

On Line, Linie 43 Punta (45% rayon, 45% nylon, 10% acrylic; 88 yards [80 m]/1.75-ounce [50-g] ball):
#23 multicolor, a combination of rich reds, purple, greens, orange, blues bouclé yarn, about 45 yards (42 m), for the headband

Classic Elite Waterspun (100% merino felted wool; 137 yards [125 m]/1.75-ounce [50-g] skein):
#5051 Tibetan Gold, about 8–10 yards (7–9 m) for flower

Needles
Size 8 (5 mm) 16-inch (40.5-cm) circular (circ) to make the headband. Size 5 (3.75 mm) to make the flower. **Adjust the needle size if necessary to obtain the correct gauge.**

Gauge
Version #1: 16 stitches and 17 rows = 3 inches (7.5 cm), on size 8 (5 mm) needles in knit 2 (k2), purl 2 (p2) rib, with 2 strands of yarn held together as one. Both gauge samples were worked back and forth in stitch pattern. Flat knitting usually has a different gauge than circular knitting, but in these small, stretchy items, the difference isn't significant.

Version #2: 14 stitches and 13 rows = 3 inches (7.5 cm), on size 8 (5 mm) needles with 2 strands of yarn held together as one

Notions
Tapestry needle; marker; US size E (3.5 mm) crochet hook for decorating the yellow flower; 5 tiny beads (optional), for decorating the center of the flower; matching sewing thread and sewing needle to attach beads.

Make the Headband

Using the circular needle and holding together 1 strand from each yarn, cast on (CO) 80 stitches (sts). Place a marker and join sts into a circle, being careful not to twist the sts. Work in rounds (rnds) of k2, p2 ribbing until the headband measures the desired width. Bind off (BO) all sts in pattern.

Make the Flower

Using smaller needles, with a single strand of yarn, CO 5 sts.

Row 1: Knit.

Rows 2,4,6,8, and 10: Purl.

Rows 3,5, and 7: Knit 1 in the front and back loops (k1f&b) at each end of the row—(11 sts at the end of row 7).

Rows 9 and 11: Knit 2 together (k2tog) at each end of row.

Row 12: P2tog, p3, p2tog—5 sts remain. Do not BO.

Leave sts on needle. Cut the yarn, leaving a 6-inch (15-cm) tail.

Join yarn and repeat (rep) the above 12 rows 6 more times. Leave yarn attached on the 7th and last petal. Each petal has a 5-st base—(35 sts).

Next Row: K2tog across the row to the last st, k1— (18 sts). Cut the yarn, leaving a 12-inch (30-cm) tail. With a tapestry needle, thread the tail through the remaining 18 sts. Pull yarn gently to gather the sts together, then fasten yarn securely by weaving through several sts on the wrong side (WS). Overlapping the flower petals, sew the edges of the petals together from the petal base upward to the widest point. Leave the upper petals free. Weave in loose ends to WS and secure.

Finishing the Flowers

Orange Flower
Using the photo at right as a guide, thread a tapestry needle with about 18 inches (46 cm) Classic Elite Montera yarn, in Pear color, and make 12 lines using long and short straight sewing stitches radiating outward from the flower center.

Yellow Flower
Decorate the flower with the Dalegarn Sisik yarn used to make the headband. Thread a tapestry needle with about 18 inches (46 cm) of the yarn and embroider a chain (see Techniques, page 116) around the outside edges of the petals as shown on headband at left in the photograph on page 51. Rethread needle as necessary. Cut yarn, leaving a 4-inch (10-cm) tail, and weave in loose ends to WS and secure.

To make the loopy center of the flower: With crochet hook and Sisik yarn, chain 16 sts (see Techniques, page 114). *Insert the hook back into the first chain formed (this will form the first loop) and chain 16 more sts*; rep instructions between * * until there are 7 loops. Pull the loops into place to form the flower center. Cut yarn, leaving a 6-inch (15-cm) tail; thread the yarn through the loop, and tighten. Attach the loop center to the flower. With matching sewing thread and needle, sew a few beads into the center, if desired.

Attaching the Flower

Using a coordinating color of yarn, thread 8 inches (20.5 cm) onto a tapestry needle. Neatly attach the flower to the headband with a few backstitches (see Techniques, page 118). With a tapestry needle, weave in loose tails to WS of work and secure.

Go to San Francisco.

Approximate Head Measurements

These measurements came from a chart in my pediatrician's office and can be used as a guide
when knitting headbands, hats, and skullcaps.

AGE	GIRLS	BOYS
12 months	18¼ inches (46.5 cm)	18½ inches (47 cm)
23 months	19 inches (48.5 cm)	19¼ inches (49 cm)
3 years	19¾ inches (50 cm)	20 inches (51 cm)
6 years	20 inches (51 cm)	20½ inches (52 cm)
8 years	20½ inches (52 cm)	20½ inches (52 cm)
10 years	21 inches (53.5 cm)	21 inches (53.5 cm)
12 years	21¼ inches (54 cm)	21½ inches (54.5 cm)
18+ years	21½ inches (54.5 cm)	22 inches (56 cm)

These are very basic measurements. Knitting stretches, and skullcaps should fit snugly.

Easy Rolled-Edge Hat

One version uses a single strand of super bulky yarn, and the second version is knit using six strands of lightweight yarn.

Finished Size
Circumference: about 19 to 20 inches (48.5–51 cm)
Height: 11 inches (28 cm) before edge rolls

Yarn
You will need about 66 yards (60 m) total of super bulky yarn for Version #1, or combine 6 strands of lightweight yarns to create a super bulky yarn. Each strand should have at least 66 yards (60 m) for Version #2, and use the same pattern and gauge.

For Version #1 hat (black, cream, and red), we used Rowan Biggy Print (100% merino wool; 33 yards [30 m]/3.5-ounce [100-g] skein):
#254 Humbug, about 66 yards (60 m)

For Version #2 hat (multicolored), we used Dalegarn Falk (100% wool; 116 yards [106 m]/1.75-ounce [50-g] skein):
#4246 Warm Burgundy, about 66 yards (60 m)

Dalegarn Freestyle (100% wool; 88 yards [80 m]/1.75-ounce [50-g] skein):
#2106 yellow, about 66 yards (60 m)

Dalegarn Daletta (100% wool; 154 yards [141 m]/1.75-ounce [50-g]) skein:
#0020 Natural, about 66 yards (60 m)

Dalegarn Heilo (100% wool; 109 yards [100 m]/1.75-ounce [50-g] skein):
#7382 Deep Teal, about 66 yards (60 m)

Raumagarn Finull Garn (100% wool; 180 yards [165 m]/1.75-ounce [50-g] skein):
#447 Blue, about 66 yards (60 m)
#408 Gold, about 66 yards (60 m)

Needles
Size 15 (10 mm) double-point (dpn), set of 5. *Adjust the needle size if necessary to obtain the correct gauge.*

Gauge
9 stitches and 11 rounds = 4 inches (10 cm) in circular stockinette stitch (St st).

Notions
Markers; tapestry needle

Make the Hat

Cast on (CO) 40 stitches (sts). Place a marker and join sts into a circle, being careful not to twist.

Edge Roll
Knit every round (rnd) until the hat measures 3 inches (8 cm) from CO edge.

Hat Body
Change to knit 2, purl 2 ribbing; work in rib until the hat measures 9½ inches (24 cm) from the CO edge.

Hat Crown
Rnd 1: (first decrease [dec] rnd) *Knit 2 (k2), purl 2 together (p2tog), k2, p2*; repeat (rep) instructions between * * to end of rnd—(35 sts remain).

Rnd 2: *K2, p1, k2, p2*; rep instructions between * * to end of rnd.

Rnd 3: (second dec rnd) *K2, p1, k2, p2tog*; rep instructions between * * to end of rnd—(30 sts).

Rnd 4: *K2, p1, k2, p1*; rep instructions between * * to end of rnd.

Rnd 5: *K2tog; rep from * to end of rnd—(15 sts).

Rnd 6: *K1, k2tog*; rep instructions between * * to end of rnd—(10 sts).

Rnd 7: *K2tog; rep from * to end of rnd—(5 sts).

Finishing

Cut the yarn, leaving a tail about 6 inches (15 cm) long. Thread a tapestry needle with yarn tail and weave through the remaining sts. Pull the yarn tail gently to draw the sts together and close the crown top. Weave the yarn to the wrong side (WS) of the work and weave through several sts to secure. With a tapestry needle, weave in loose yarn tails to the WS of work and secure.

Walk on the Wild Side Slipper Socks

Version #1 of these toe-up slipper socks uses nine gorgeous LaLana Wools colors to brighten your day. Don't be afraid to knit unmatched yet coordinated slippers. Version #2 of this slipper sock is knit in one color and has a fringe of LaLana Wools' Karakul Tailspun around the top. The skull charm sewn along the top edge makes it a perfect choice for your favorite Goth teen.

Finished Size
Length of foot: 8½ (10) inches (21.5 [25.5] cm)
Length of leg, from bottom of heel to top of sock leg: 9 inches (23 cm). Version #1 will be slightly shorter after the top edge rolls forward.

Yarn
To make the sizes shown here, you will need:
For Version #1, about ¼–½ ounce (14 g), 16 to 17 yards (15–16 m), of 9 colors.
For Version #2, about 150 yards (137 m) total of medium-weight yarn worked at the recommended gauge and about 1 to 2 yards (1–2 m) of fuzzy novelty yarn for the trim.

For Version #1 (stripes), we used LaLana Wools Forever Random Blends (100% wool; worsted weight, 82 yards [75 m]/2-ounce [57-g] skein):
Color A—Primavera, 16–17 yards (15–16 m)

LaLana Wools Forever Random Obverse Blends (60% Romney wool, 40% yearling mohair; 82 yards [75 m]/ 2-ounce [57-g] skein):

16 to 17 yards (15–16 m) in each of the following colors:
Color B—Sweet Lorraine
Color C—Pastoral
Color E—TeRosada
Color F—Bayeta
Color H—Green Apple

LaLana Wools Silk (100% silk; 37½ yards [34 m]/ 1-ounce [28.5-g] skein):
16 to 17 yards (15–16 m) in each of the following colors:
Color D—Sweet Pea
Color G—Lupine
Color I—Dark Madder

For Version #2 (almost black with hairy fringe), we used LaLana Wools Forever Random Obverse Blends

(60% Romney wool, 40% yearling mohair; worsted weight, 82 yards [75 m]/2-ounce [57-g] skein):
Zulu Prince, 150 yards (137 m)
Karakul Tailspun (100% wool; 1 ounce [28 g] minimum)
Natural, at least 1 ounce (the fringe lengths vary)

Needles
US size 8 (5 mm) double-point (dpn), set of 5. ***Adjust the needle size if necessary to obtain the correct gauge.***

Gauge
14 stitches and 19 rounds = 4 inches (10 cm) in circular stockinette stitch (St st) (knit each round)

Notions
Crochet hook, US size H/8 (5 mm); stitch markers; tapestry needle; about 18 inches (46 cm) smooth waste cotton yarn for provisional (temporary) cast-on. To give these socks durability and help prevent slipping, attach one- or two-piece leather soles to the bottoms (see Resources, page 121).

Version #1 color sequence:
Color A—Sonrisa
Color B—Primavera
Color C—Pastoral
Color D—Sweet Pea
Color E—TeRosada
Color F—Bayeta
Color G—Lupine
Color H—Green Apple
Color A—Sonrisa
Color I—Dark Madder
Color F—Bayeta
Color H—Green Apple
Color B—Primavera
Color G—Lupine
Color A—Sonrisa
Color H—Green Apple
Color E—TeRosada
Color F—Bayeta

● ● ●
Stash-Busting Tip
If you knit both of these toe-up socks simultaneously on two separate sets of double-point needles, it is easy to judge exactly how long the leg portion can be, depending on the amount of yarn you have available.

Make the Slipper Socks

Toe

Both Versions: With crochet hook and the waste yarn, chain 12 stitches (sts) to make a provisional (temporary) crochet chain cast-on (CO) (see Techniques, page 115).

Row 1: Join Color A for Version #1 and the main yarn for Version #2, and, using the beginning end of the crochet chain, pick up 8 sts from the crochet chain. Work in rows, back and forth in St st, for 4 rows. Beginning at the knotted end of the waste yarn pull the end out of the last crochet st and then remove the provisional CO, inserting a dpn into the live sts to create a seamless beginning (see Techniques, page 115).

One dpn holds 8 sts at one end of the 4 rows, and a second dpn holds 8 sts at the other end of the 4 rows. Fold the 4 rows in half and then slip 4 sts purlwise (pwise) onto each of 4 dpns—(16 sts). Place a marker (pm) on the needle where the working yarn is attached. From this point on, you'll be working in rounds (rnds), and the marker will identify the beginning of the rnd and *Needle #1.*

Rnd 1:

Needle #1: K1, with the tip of the right needle, lift the st below the st on the left needle and knit it. Knit the remaining sts on the needle—(5 sts);

Needle #2: Knit to within 1 st of the end; with the left needle, lift the st below the st on the right needle and knit it, k1—(5 sts);

Needle #3: Work same as *Needle #1;*

Needle #4: Work same as *Needle #2.*

20 sts total.

Rnd 2: Knit.

Repeat (rep) these two rnds 1 (2) more times—(24 [28] sts). There are 6 (7) sts on each needle.

Work even in circular St st (knit every rnd) for both versions until the foot measures approximately 6 (6½) inches (15 [16½] cm) from the toe. This will be the point where the leg meets the top of the foot. In Version #1, you'll also be changing colors randomly at the beginning of every 2–6 rnds, rotating through the color order listed on the previous page. Or, select your choice of colors and stripe widths. Each rnd ends after completing *Needle #4.* When foot is desired length, begin the heel.

Heel

The sts on *Needles #1 and #2* are the sole of the sock. The sts on *Needles #3 and #4* are for the instep.

Next Rnd: *Needle #1:* Knit 1, lift the st below the st to the left and knit it; knit to the end of the needle—(7 [8] sts);

Needle #2: Knit to within 1 st of the end; lift the st below the st just knitted and knit the lifted st, k1—(7 [8] sts);

Needles #3 and #4: Knit.

Next Rnd: Knit all sts.

Work these 2 rnds 4 (4) times—(32 [36] sts).

Needles #1 and #2 each have 10 (11) sts (the sole sts); *Needles #3 and #4* (the instep sts) each have 6 (7) sts.

Turn the Heel

Place all the heel sts on one needle by knitting 6 (7) sts from *Needle #1* onto *Needle #4.* Heel Needle: Using the free dpn, ssk (see Abbreviations, page 120), knit 2 (2) sts from *Needle #1* and knit 4 (4) sts from *Needle #2* onto the heel needle. Slip the remaining 6 (7) sts from *Needle #2* onto *Needle #3.* There should be 12 (14) sts held on each of *Needles #3 and #4.* There are now 7 (7) sts on the heel needle. Work the heel back and forth in St st on these 7 sts as follows:

Row 1: Wrong side (WS). Purl 2 together (p2tog), purl across the row. Turn.

Row 2: Right side (RS). Ssk, knit across the row. Turn.

Rep these 2 rows until 4 sts remain; end after completing a Row 1 (WS). Turn work.

Next Row: (RS) Sl 1, knit across the heel. Pick up 4 sts by knitting along the decrease (dec) edge. Turn.

Next Row: (WS) Sl 1 pwise. Purl back across the heel and pick up 4 sts pwise along the other dec edge—(12 [12] sts) on the heel needle. Turn.

Heel Flap

Begin knitting the heel flap, working away from the foot and toward the leg, and, *at the same time,* working together 1 st from the adjacent instep needle with 1 st from the heel sts each time you turn the work. *Note:* 12 sts remain on the heel needles as you work these rows.

Row 1: (RS) Sl 1, knit across the row to the last st, sl the last st pwise to right needle, then sl 1 pwise from the next needle to the right needle; return both slipped sts pwise to left needle and then knit the 2 slipped sts together (k2tog). Turn.

Row 2: (WS) Sl 1, purl across the row to the last st, sl the last st to next needle on the left, then p2tog with the right needle. Turn.

Rep these two rows 6 times; end after completing a WS Row 2—(12 sts on the heel needle and 6 [8] sts on each instep needle). Turn the work so RS is facing and resume working in rnds. As you work the first rnd, to eliminate a gap in the work on each side of the heel sts, *lift the st below the first st on the left needle, and knit the lifted st

together with the first st on left needle, knit across the remaining sts on the first needle; repeat from * at the beginning of the next needle to close the gap on the other side of the heel; knit all the sts on the last two needles to complete the rnd. Adjust the sts so there are 6 (7) sts on each of the four needles. For Version #1, continue changing colors, creating a stripe pattern. Work evenly for both versions until sock leg is almost as long as you want the sock to be, about 5 inches (12.5 cm) for Version #1, the striped socks, and about 7 inches (18 cm) for Version #2.

Sock Top

Version #1: To create the striped ridge top:

Rnd 1: Change color and knit rnd.

Rnds 2–3: Purl.

Rnd 4: Change to another color, knit rnd.

Rnds 5–6: Purl.

Rnd 7: Change to another color, knit rnd.

Rnds 8–9: Purl.

Bind off (BO) loosely.

Version #2: To create the fringed top, when leg measures about 7 inches (18 cm) or desired length, hold several strands of the Karakul long tail yarn in front of the needle. (The Karakul long tail yarn is held in front of the work throughout.)

Insert the right needle above the long tail yarn; bring the working yarn under and around the long tail yarn, securing it into the first st on *Needle #1* and knit the st. Secure the long tail yarn in this manner every 4th st, bringing the working yarn under and around each section of long tail yarn. Roll the top of the sock down over the top edge of the long tail yarn. Thread a tapestry needle with 18 inches (48 cm) and sew the top edge in place. Trim the ends of the long tail yarn if necessary. Add a bead or two to the top edge if desired.

Finishing

Using a tapestry needle, weave in ends to WS and secure. Attach the leather soles if desired, following the instructions on the package. Take a walk on the wild side.

Striped Skullcap

This skullcap can be made as subdued or wild as you want.

Color Chart

Finished Size
Circumference: 18 inches (46 cm)
Length: 7 inches (18 cm)

Yarn
You will need about 175 yards (160 m) total of fine yarn, divided by as many colors as you choose to use. The hat featured here uses about 20 yards (18 m) each in 6 colors, and the hat weighs about 2 ounces (57 g).

We used Weaving Southwest sportweight hand-dyed wool (100% wool; 375 yards (343 m)/4-ounce [113-g] skein):
About 20 yards (18 m) of each of the following:
Color A—Black
Color B—Emerald
Color C—Grape
Color D—Turquoise
Color E—Sangre
Color F—Butter

Needles
US size 1 (2.25 mm) 16-inch (40.5-cm) circular (circ); US size 2 (2.75 mm) 16-inch circ; US size 2 (2.75 mm) double-point (dpn), set of 4 or 5. **Adjust the needle size if necessary to obtain the correct gauge.**

Gauge
31 stitches and 39 rows = 4 inches (10 cm) in stockinette stitch (St st) on larger-size needles

Notions
Markers; tapestry needle; an assortment of beads; needle for threading beads to form the beaded tassel; about 1 yard (1 m) embroidery thread to use if the yarn is too thick to fit through bead holes.

Note
At the beginning of the round, use a stitch marker in a different color than the color used for the other markers.

Key
- ■ Black (color A)
- ■ Emerald (color B)
- ■ Grape (color C)
- ■ Turquoise (color D)
- ■ Sangre (color E)
- □ Butter (color F)
- □ Pattern repeat frame
- · Purl on RS
- □ Knit on RS in appropriate color as shown in chart

Make the Striped Skullcap

Using the smaller-size circular needle, cast on (CO) 125 sts with Color C. Place a marker to indicate beginning of round (rnd) and join work into circle, being careful not to twist the stitches (sts). Begin Color Chart, working 13 rounds (rnds) in knit 1, purl 1 ribbing. Change to larger-size needles and work in circ St st using colors as shown on the chart.

Crown Shaping
When work measures about 5 inches (12.5 cm) from CO (row 49 of chart), place a marker after every 25 sts (this includes the marker at the beginning of the rnds). Continue using Color Chart and begin shaping as follows: knit 2 together (k2tog) right after the first marker and then k2tog after each remaining marker on every rnd until 5 sts remain. Change to dpns when necessary. Cut the yarn, leaving a 6-inch (15-cm) tail.

Finishing

Thread tapestry needle with yarn tail and weave through the remaining sts. Pull yarn gently to close the hat crown. Weave yarn tails to wrong side (WS) of work and secure.

Bead Tassel
String several beads on a piece of yarn or embroidery floss to form a bead tassel at the top of the hat. Make sure the tassel isn't longer than the hat, or it will bump into the wearer's eyes. The bead tassel is not recommended on hats for toddlers or babies.

Checkered Skullcap

A slight variation from the Striped Skullcap, this one is perfect when you're feeling checky.

Color Chart

◄ Begin decreases

Finished Size
Circumference: 20 inches (51 cm)
Length: 7½ inches (19 cm)

Yarn
You will need about 175 yards (160 m) total of fine yarn, divided by as many colors as you choose to use. The hat featured here uses about 20 yards (18 m) each in 6 colors, and the hat weighs about 2 ounces (57 g).

We used Weaving Southwest sportweight hand-dyed wool (100% wool; 375 yards (343 m)/4-ounce [113-g] skein):
About 20 yards (18 m) of each of the following:
Color A—Black
Color B—Emerald
Color C—Grape
Color D—Turquoise
Color E—Sangre
Color F—Butter

Needles
US size 1 (2.25 mm) 16-inch (40.5-cm) circular (circ); US size 2 (2.75 mm) 16-inch circ; US size 2 (2.75 mm) double-point (dpn), set of 4 or 5. **Adjust the needle size if necessary to obtain the correct gauge.**

Gauge
33 stitches (sts) and 32 rounds = 4 inches (10 cm) in circular stockinette stitch (St st) on larger-size needles

Notions
Markers; tapestry needle

Note
In the following crown shaping, the decreases (dec) alter the checkered pattern on some rnds. To preserve the pattern in the rest of the work after a dec is made, simply use whatever color maintains the pattern for the next st, even when it means the dec and the next st are worked in the same color.

Make the Skullcap

Using the smaller-size circular needle, cast on (CO) 150 sts with Color B. Place marker and join work into a circle, being careful not to twist the stitches (sts). Follow Color Chart, working 10 rounds (rnds) in knit 1, purl 1 ribbing as shown. Change to larger-size needles and work in circ St st (knit every rnd) following the color chart.

Key

■ Black (color A)
■ Emerald (color B)
■ Grape (color C)
▨ Turquoise (color D)
▨ Sangre (color E)
□ Butter (color F)
□ Pattern repeat frame
⊡ Purl on RS
□ Knit on RS in appropriate color as shown in chart

Crown Shaping

When the work measures about 5½ inches (14 cm) from CO edge (row 38), place one marker after every 25 sts (this number includes the marker at the beginning of the rnds). Continuing to follow the color chart, work shaping as follows: knit 2 together (k2tog) right after the first marker and after every marker thereafter. Continue decreasing, switching to dpns when necessary, until 6 sts remain.

Finishing

Cut the yarn, leaving a tail about 6 inches (15 cm) long. Thread tapestry needle with yarn tail and weave through the remaining sts. Pull the yarn tail gently to draw the sts together and close the crown top. Weave in the yarn to the wrong side (WS) of the work and secure. Weave in loose yarn tails to the WS of work and secure.

for home

When thinking of ways to knit up your stash, don't limit yourself to wearable projects. Use your yarn to make something nice for your home. In this chapter, you will find patterns for a rug, an afghan, and a pillow. Also, check out the whimsical miniature Christmas stockings, which are great to use for decorating or for holding a very special gift!

If your stash contains many colors, tie them together with a neutral color such as gray or black, as in the Felted Patchwork Rug (page 74) and the Amish-Inspired Afghan (page 76). The Trellis Pillow (page 70) demonstrates how monochromatic hues of one color (in this case, red) can be used to create a sophisticated look.

While there is not a definitive pattern for coasters in the book, they are a great way to use up a small amount of yarn. Simply knit 4-inch (10-cm) squares. Or, if using 100 percent wool, try felting them. Begin by knitting 5-inch (12.5-cm) squares, then follow the felting instructions on page 75. Coordinate the coaster colors, including stripes and trims, and tie together with coordinating yarn to present them as a great hostess gift.

Mini Christmas Stockings

Quick to make, you can knit these up all year long in preparation for the holiday season. If you haven't turned a sock heel before, give the concept a try using these step-by-step instructions on a miniature scale. Christmas stockings are a good way to deliver gift certificates and, unlike a pair of regular socks, you only have to make one!

Finished Size
Height: 5¾ inches (14.5 cm)
Length of foot: 3½ inches (9 cm)
Width of top of stocking: 2 inches (5 cm)

Yarn
You will need about 30 yards (28 m) total of medium-weight yarn to make each miniature stocking, using the same stitch pattern and gauge. The colors and amounts are included with the instructions for each specific stocking.

We used Harrisville New England Knitters Highland (100% wool; worsted-weight 2-ply, 200 yards [183 m]/3.5-ounce [100-g] skein).

Needles
US size 2 (2.75 mm) double-point (dpn), set of 4.
Adjust the needle size if necessary to obtain the correct gauge.

Gauge
12 stitches and 19 rounds = 2 inches (5 cm) in circlar stockinette stitch (St st)

Notions
Tapestry needle; markers; stitch holder or waste cotton yarn to use as holder. When making a stocking with bead trim, you will need small beads, the size of your choosing, beading needle, and beading thread. For a stocking that includes a button, you will need a decorative button about ½ inch (1.3 cm) in diameter, sewing needle, and thread. For a stocking with pre-beaded trim, you will need to make or purchase about ½ yard (46 cm) of prebeaded trim.

Notes
1. Look through your current supply of beads, buttons, and other accessories to trim the mini stockings.

2. Slip stitches as if to purl (sl pwise).

Basic Cuffed Stocking

Follow these directions for all the variations.

Cuff
Cast on (CO) 25 stitches (sts). Arrange sts so there are 9 sts on one needle and 8 on each of 2 needles. Place a marker to identify beginning of round (rnd) and join work into circle, being careful not to twist the sts. Knit 9 rnds. Purl 1 rnd to form top fold line of the cuff.

Fold Line and Stocking
Turn work to wrong side (WS) (from this point on, this side is the right side [RS]). Continue to knit in rnds; *at the same time,* decrease (dec) 1 st in the first rnd—(24 sts). When stocking leg measures 4 inches (10 cm) from the top of the fold line, divide sts for the heel.

Heel Flap
(Worked back and forth in rows on 2 needles.) K6, turn work, and purl back over these same 6 sts, place a marker, and then purl the next 6 sts—(12 sts). Place the remaining 12 sts on holder for instep.

Working back and forth on heel sts only, slip (sl) the first st of every row and work 13 rows in St st, ending with a purl row.

Turn the Heel (short rows)
Row 1: (RS) K7, knit 2 together (k2tog), k1, turn.

Row 2: Sl 1, p3, purl 2 together (p2tog), p1, turn.

Row 3: Sl 1, k4, k2tog, k1, turn.

Row 4: Sl 1, p5, p2tog, p1—8 sts remain on needle.

Set Up the Heel Gusset
With empty needle, knit across 4 heel sts, place a marker to identify beginning of rnd; using another empty needle, knit across the next 4 heel sts; using the same needle, pick up 6 sts along side edge of heel flap. Slip 12 instep sts from holder onto a free needle, and, using another empty needle, knit across the 12 instep sts. Using the 4th needle, pick up 6 sts down the other side of heel, and using this same needle, knit across remaining 4 heel sts—(32 sts). The beginning of the rnd is now the center of the heel.

Shape the Gusset

Rnd 1: Knit.

Rnd 2: (dec rnd)

Needle #1: Knit to within 3 sts of end of needle, k2tog, k1;

Needle #2: K12 instep sts;

Needle #3: K1, ssk (see Abbreviations, page 120), knit to end of rnd.

Repeat (rep) last 2 rnds until 24 sts remain. Knit 10 rnds for foot.

Shape the Toe

Rnd 1: (dec rnd)

Needle #1: Knit to last 3 sts, k2tog, k1;

Needle #2: K1, ssk, knit to last 3 sts, k2tog, k1;

Needle #3: K1, ssk, knit to end of rnd.

Rnd 2: Knit.

Rep these 2 rnds once. Then rep Rnd 1 (dec rnd) 2 more times—8 sts remain.

Finishing

Cut yarn, leaving a 6-inch (15-cm) tail. Thread tapestry needle with yarn tail and weave through the remaining sts. Pull gently to close toe opening, secure, and fasten off. Weave in loose ends to the WS of work and secure.

Hanger

Knot together three 8-inch (20-cm) strands of yarn, using an overhand knot about ½ inch (1.3 cm) from the end of each strand. Braid the strands together until the braid is about 4 inches (10 cm) from knot or desired length. Knot the ends together with an overhand knot, same as beginning knot, and trim uneven ends. Fold the braid in half and, using a tapestry needle threaded with yarn, attach the hanger to the stocking.

Make the Cuffed Green Stocking with Tractor Button

#8 Hemlock, about 30 yards (28 m)

Knit the entire stocking following the basic instructions. Sew decorative button to cuff, if desired.

Make the Two-Tone Green Stocking with Beads

Color A—#68 Olive, about 5 yards (4.5 m)
Color B—#9 Evergreen, about 25 yards (23 m)

Follow the basic instructions to make the stocking, using Color A for the cuff and, beginning at the fold line, Color B for the remainder of stocking. Sew 12 coral disks and 12 turquoise-colored seed beads around the top of the stocking. Make the hanger out of about 18 red and 18 turquoise seed beads strung on a piece of yarn.

Make the Red and White Stocking

Color A—#44 White, about 5 yards (4.5 m)
Color B—#2 Red, about 25 yards (23 m)

Follow the basic instructions, using Color A for the cuff, but do not turn the work at the fold line. Change to Color B and simply continue with the remaining instructions. With sewing needle and thread, attach the beaded ribbon trim to the stocking with whipstitch (see Techniques, page 118) under the cuff.

Make the Red, Fuchsia, and Orange Stocking

Color A—#74 Rose, about 6 yards (5.5 m)
Color B—#35 Chianti, about 8 yards (7.5 m)
Color C—#65 Poppy, about 12 yards (11 m)
Color D—#2 Red, about 4 yards (3.7 m)

Following the basic instructions, CO using Color A. Knit 2 rnds. Purl 1 rnd with Color B. Knit 2 rnds with Color B. Purl 1 rnd with Color C. Knit 2 rnds with Color C. Purl 1 rnd with Color D. Knit 2 rnds with Color D. Purl 1 rnd with Color A. Knit 2 rnds with Color A. Turn work. Continue to knit in rnds, working the next 4 rnds with Color C; *at the same time,* dec 1 st in first rnd only. Knit 3 rnds with Color D. Knit 2 rnds with Color B. Knit 4 rnds with Color A. Knit 3 rnds with Color C. Knit 4 rnds with Color B. Knit 2 rnds with Color D. Work heel in Color C as you follow the directions for shaping the rest of the stocking. When you have formed a 5–rnd stripe of Color A on the front of the foot, switch to Color B for 5 rnds, switch to Color D for 3 rnds, switch to Color B for 5 rnds, and finish the toe of the stocking with Color C.

Make the Blue and Orange Striped Stocking

About 10 yards (91.44 m) in each of 3 colors:
Color A—#13 Peacock
Color B—#17 Bermuda Blue
Color C—#66 Melon

Following the basic instructions, CO with Color A. For cuff, knit 1 rnd in Color A, knit 1 rnd in Color B, knit 1 rnd in Color C. Repeat these 3 rnds twice more. Purl 1 rnd with Color C to form the turning ridge of the cuff. Turn work to WS (this side of work is now the RS) and knit 15 rnds in Color C. Knit 5 rnds in Color B. Knit 5 rnds Color A. Knit 5 rnds Color C. Knit 5 rnds Color B. Work heel in Color A, and follow the basic instructions above for shaping the rest of the stocking. When you have formed a 5–rnd stripe of Color A on the front of the foot, switch to Color C for 5 rnds, switch to Color B for 5 rnds, switch to Color A for 5 rnds, and finish the toe of the stocking with Color C.

● ● ●
Stash-Busting Tip

Think small. Little projects such as these stockings make a perfect palette for trying out interesting color combinations.

Trellis Pillow

Red has been my favorite color since I knew the names of colors, so it wasn't surprising I had many hues of it in my stash. I used several reds in this pillow along with a judicious splash of yellow to help spark them up and pull the colors together. Perhaps you have a favorite color and your stash has several varieties of the same color family. The center motif is worked with a stranded Fair Isle pattern, but you can choose to leave the center panel plain or follow the chart using a vertical duplicate stitch (see Techniques, page 117) after the pillow face is finished.

Finished Size
Width: 19 inches (48.5 cm)
Length: 24 inches (61 cm)

Yarn
You will need about 544 yards (497 m) total of lightweight yarn, using the same stitch pattern and gauge.

We used Classic Elite Yarns Provence (100% Mercerized Egyptian Cotton; 205 yards [187 m]/3.5-ounce [100-g] skein) in the following colors:

Color A—#2658 Geranium, 232 yards (212 m)
Color B—#2627 French Red, 96 yards (88 m)
Color C—#2623 Biddeford Shrimp, 28 yards (26 m)
Color D—#2695 Watermelon, 64 yards (59 m)
Color E—#2661 Summer Wheat, 124 yards (113 m)

Needles
US size 4 (3.5 mm). **Adjust the needle size if necessary to obtain the correct gauge.**

Gauge
21 stitches and 32 rows = 4 inches (10 cm) in stockinette stitch (St st)

Notions
Bobbins; tapestry needle; US size F/5 (3.75 mm) crochet hook; 2 pieces of red material, about 20 inches x 25 inches (51 cm x 63.5 cm) each, to make the inner pillow form; 20 ounces (567 g) polyester filling; piece of red corduroy or other sturdy fabric to use for pillow backing, about 20 inches x 25 inches (51 cm x 63.5 cm); sewing machine and sewing thread to sew the inner pillow together; sewing needle to sew the pillow top to the back.

Notes
1. The intarsia stripes will require a minimum of 8 bobbins or yarn butterflies. The 6 single-stitch stripes in Colors E and C can use long strands of yarn without winding on bobbins. Or, these stripes can be added later using vertical duplicate stitch or embroidered chain stitch (see Techniques, pages 117 and 116).

2. The pillow shown here has a fabric back; however, a knitted pillow back is an option if you have plenty of suitable yarns in your stash. It could be worked in one color, a series of stripes, or the same pattern used for the front. A knitted back will require twice the amount of yarn listed. If you choose to knit the back, then finish the pillow by crocheting both pieces together.

3. If you have a sewing machine, you can use it instead of the backstitch to sew back and front pieces together.

Seed Stitch Pattern

(worked over odd number of stitches)

Row 1: P1, k1, p1.

Repeat (rep) Row 1 for pattern stitch (st).

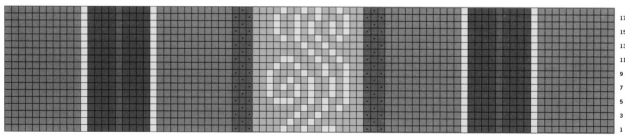

RS rows: Begin chart at right edge, work across row from right to left, changing colors as shown—88 stitches.

WS rows: Begin at left edge, work across row from left to right.

Work Rows 1–18 ten times—180 rows.

Key

■ Color A—#2658 Geranium: Knit on RS; purl on WS

■ Color B—#2627 French Red: Knit on RS; purl on WS

■ Color C—#2623 Biddeford Shrimp: Knit on RS; purl on WS

■ Color C—#2623 Biddeford Shrimp: Purl on RS; knit on WS

■ Color D—#2695 Watermelon: Knit on RS; purl on WS

□ Color E—#2662 Summer Wheat: Knit on RS; purl on WS

□ Repeat frame

Make the Pillow Top

Cast on (CO) 88 sts using Color A. Following the intarsia and Fair Isle chart on page 72, add the other yarn colors on bobbins and repeat the 18 chart rows for a total of 10 times—(180 rows). The pillow front measures about 23 inches (58.5 cm) from CO edge before the crochet borders are added. Work the chart stitch repeats as follows:

Row 1: (RS) Begin at lower right edge of chart. *Side patterns:* *k11 with Color A, k1 with Color E, k4 with Color B, k1 with Color C, k4 with Color B, k1 with Color E, k11 with Color A*; *Center patterns:* Work 3 sts in seed st pattern (patt) with Color C, work 16 sts in Fair Isle patt with Colors D and E according to chart, work 3 sts in seed st with Color C; *Side patterns:* repeat side patt instructions from * to *.

Row 2: (WS) Begin on second row of chart. *Side patterns:* *p11 with Color A, p1 with Color E, p4 with Color B, p1 with Color C, p4 with Color B, p1 with Color E, p11 with Color A*; *Center patterns:* Work 3 sts in seed st, purl the 16 Fair Isle sts using colors as shown, work 3 sts in seed st; *Side patterns:* Rep from * to *.

These 2 rows are the first 2 rows shown on the chart. Work the 18 chart rows 10 times for a total of 180 rows to complete the pillow front. Bind off (BO) all sts. With tapestry needle, weave in loose yarn tails to the WS of the work along the stripe edges and secure.

Using the crochet hook and Color E, work a row of single crochet (sc) (see Techniques, page 114) around the outside of the pillow; *at the same time,* work 3 sc in each corner stitch to smoothly round the corners and prevent puckering. Leaving Color E attached, join Color A and work 1 rnd of sc. With Color E, work a final rnd of sc. Cut yarns, leaving 4-inch (10-cm) tails, and weave in loose ends on WS.

Wet pillow top, block flat to 19 x 24 inches (48.5 x 61 cm), and let dry thoroughly.

Make the Inner Pillow

Cut two pieces of fabric about 20 x 25 inches (51 x 63.5 cm), which includes a ½-inch (1.3-cm) seam allowance around all four edges. Place fabric right sides (RS) together, and pin along the ½-inch (1.3-cm) seam allowance. With sewing needle and matching thread, sew the two fabric pieces together using the backstitch seam method (see Techniques, page 118), leaving a 6-inch (15-cm) opening across the top.

Turn the pillow right-side out and insert polyester filling. When the inner pillow is filled to desired capacity, turn in the top opening seam allowance to the wrong side (WS) and whipstitch (see Techniques, page 118) the opening together.

Finishing

Cut pillow-backing fabric to match the knitted pillow front, plus a ½-inch (1.3-cm) seam allowance around all four sides. Fold and press seam allowance to WS. With WS of knitted front and fabric backing facing together, use sewing needle and matching thread to whipstitch around three sides, leaving the crochet borders free. Weave in all loose ends to WS and secure. Insert the inner pillow and whipstitch the last side closed.

● ● ●

Stash-Busting Tip

Rows of single crochet are simple to add around the outside edge of any knitted piece; they create a decorative border and stop the edges from curling.

Felted Patchwork Rug

This felted rug starts with just six garter stitch squares, each knit diagonally. The squares are then sewn together and crocheted around the outside edge. Each square is portable, making this a perfect project for knitting on the go.

Finished Size
Each square: 8 inches x 8 inches square (20.5 x 20.5 cm)
Rug before felting: 21 inches x 27 inches (53.5 cm x 68.5 cm)
Rug after felting: 16 inches x 25 inches (40.5 cm x 63.5 cm)

Yarn
You will need about 810 yards (740 m) total of bulky weight wool yarn. (Superwash wools, synthetics, and cotton yarns will not work in this felted pattern.)

We used Reynolds Lopi (100% Icelandic wool; 110 yards [101 m]/3.5-ounce [100-g] skein):
Color A—#57 Gray, 330 yards (302 m)
Color B—#332 Antique Gold, 80 yards (73 m)
Color C—#389 Burnt Red, 80 yards (73 m)
Color D—#240 Golden Green, 80 yards (73 m)
Color E—#215 Plum, 80 yards (73 m)
Color F—#104 Terra Cotta, 80 yards (73 m)
Color G—#98 Cadet Blue, 80 yards (73 m)

Needles
US size 11 (8 mm). **Adjust the needle size if necessary to obtain the correct gauge.**

Gauge (before felting)
10 stitches and 20 rows = 4 inches (10 cm) in garter stitch

Notions
US size Q (16 mm) crochet hook; tapestry needle

Note
When a knit wool piece is washed in hot water with lots of agitation, felt is created. The fibers lock together under these conditions to form a dense, heavy fabric. As you may have discovered the hard way if you've accidentally washed a sweater in hot water, felt is forever.

Make the Rug

Using 1 strand of Color A held together with 1 strand of Color B, cast on (CO) 1 stitch (st).

Row 1: (RS) Increase (inc) 1 st by knitting into the front and then the back loop of the same st (k1f&b)—(2 sts).

Rows 2–26: Work in garter st (knit every row) as follows: Knit 1, k1f&b, knit to end of row—(27 sts).

Cut Color B leaving a 4-inch (10 cm) tail to weave in later.

Row 27: (RS) Join Color C, and with 1 strand of A and 1 strand of C held together as one, k27 sts.

Row 28: K1, knit 2 sts together (k2tog); knit to end of row —(26 sts).

Rows 29–54: Continue k2tog decreasing (dec) at the beginning of every row (work dec using the second and third sts from the edge as you did on Row 28), until 1 st remains. Cut the yarns, leaving a 6-inch (15-cm) tail, and pull the tails through the remaining loop to secure— (1 square completed).

Follow the instructions for Rows 1–54 to make the remaining 5 squares, changing colors as follows:

Square 2: 1 strand each of Colors A and D for the first half; 1 strand each of Colors A and E for the second half.

Square 3: 1 strand each Colors A and G; 1 strand each Colors A and F.

Square 4: 1 strand each Colors A and D; 1 strand each Colors A and F.

Square 5: 1 strand each Colors A and G; 1 strand each Colors A and C.

Square 6: 1 strand each Colors A and B; 1 strand each Colors A and E.

Finishing

With a tapestry needle, weave in loose yarn tails to the wrong side (WS) of work and secure.

With 2 strands of Color A threaded on a tapestry needle, whipstitch (see Techniques, page 118) the squares together as shown on schematic at right. Make sure the squares are sewn together closely so they felt together as one fabric.

With a crochet hook and two strands of Color A held together as one, work 5 rounds of single crochet (sc) (see Techniques, page 114) around the outside edges of the rug; *at the same time,* work 3 sc in each corner stitch to smoothly round the corners and prevent puckering. With a tapestry needle, weave in loose yarn tails to the WS of work and secure.

Felt the Rug

Place the rug in an old pillowcase. (Do not add towels or other items in the washing machine, as they can shed lint, which easily gets trapped in the felt.) Fill the washing machine with hot water and add a small amount of mild detergent. Add the rug in its bag and start the machine on a normal agitation cycle. Once the wash cycle is complete, check to see if the rug is felted sufficiently. Felting is complete when the stitches are obscured and the rug has shrunk. The amount of time it takes to complete the felting process varies from machine to machine. The rug shown here required two full wash cycles.

Fill the machine with cold water to rinse, and remove any detergent residue. Rinsing in cold water hardens the felt and creates a firmer fabric. Remove the rug from the rinse water and squeeze out the water by hand. Roll the rug in several heavy bath towels to eliminate as much excess water as possible. Pull and stretch the edges into shape as necessary. Sandwich the rug between two dry towels and then place something heavy on top to help flatten curled edges and absorb additional moisture. Remove the towels and let rug air-dry completely.

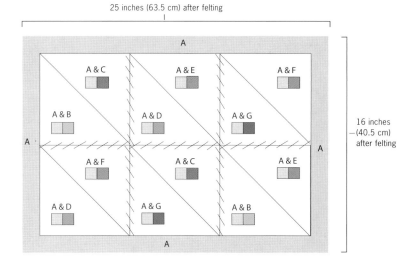

25 inches (63.5 cm) after felting

16 inches (40.5 cm) after felting

A & C · A & E · A & F
A & B · A & D · A & G
A & F · A & C · A & E
A & D · A & G · A & B

Key

Color A—#27 Gray

Color B—#322 Antique Gold

Color C—#189 Burnt Red

Color D—#340 Golden Green

Color E—#213 Plum

Color F—#104 Terra Cotta

Color G—#98 Cadet Blue

Amish-Inspired Afghan

The inspiration for this afghan started with my daughter's Girl Scout Troop, which I lead. As beginner knitters, the scouts in the troop each knit a square, and then I knit the squares together with bands of black. In the case of this afghan, the squares are knit into the afghan as part of the design, which is much easier and requires no assembly afterward.

Finished Size

Width: 37 inches (94 cm)
Length: 57½ inches (146 cm)

Yarn

You will need about 1970 yards (1801 m) total of medium-weight yarn, using the same stitch pattern and gauge. You will need 950 yards of the main color. Make sure the yarns you choose get the same gauge and call for similar cleaning methods.

We used Brown Sheep Yarn Company Lamb's Pride Worsted (85% wool, 15% mohair; 190 yards [173 m], 4-ounce [113-g] skein):
Color A—M05 Onyx, 950 yards (850 m)
Color B—M52 Spruce, 85 yards (78 m)
Color C—M83 Raspberry, 85 yards (78 m)
Color D—M58 Ink Blue, 85 yards (78 m)
Color E—M51 Winter Blue, 85 yards (78 m)
Color F—M69 Old Sage, 85 yards (78 m)
Color G—M102 Orchid Twist, 85 yards (78 m)
Color H—M22 Autumn Harvest, 85 yards (78 m)
Color I—M65 Sapphire, 85 yards (78 m)
Color J—M68 Pine Tree, 85 yards (78 m)
Color K—M25 Garnet, 85 yards (78 m)
Color L—M75 Blue Heirloom, 85 yards (78 m)
Color M—M14 Sunburst Gold, 85 yards (78 m)

Needles

US size 8 (5 mm) circular (circ), about 32 to 40 inches (81.5–101.5 cm) long. **Adjust the needle size if necessary to obtain the correct gauge.**

Gauge

17 stitches and 32 rows = 4 inches (10 cm) in garter stitch

Notions

Tapestry needle

Note

If counting ridges, remember that each garter stitch ridge equals 2 rows.

Make the Afghan

Using Color A, cast on (CO) 160 stitches (sts). Work in garter st (knit every row) for 40 rows.

Row 41: With Color A, knit 20 sts; with Color B, knit 40 sts; with Color C, knit 40 sts; with Color D, knit 40 sts; with Color A, knit 20 sts.

Row 42: With Color A, knit 20 sts; with Color D, knit 40 sts; with Color C, knit 40 sts; with Color B, knit 40 sts; with Color A, knit 20 sts.

Rows 43–120 (78 rows): Repeat Row 41 on odd-numbered rows and Row 42 on even-numbered rows.

Rows 121–140 (20 rows): With Color A, work in garter st.

Row 141: With Color A, knit 20 sts; with Color E, knit 40 sts; with Color F, knit 40 sts; with Color G, knit 40 sts; with Color A, knit 20 sts.

Row 142: With Color A, knit 20 sts; with Color G, knit 40 sts; with Color F, knit 40 sts; with Color E, knit 40 sts; with Color A, knit 20 sts.

Rows 143–220 (78 rows): Repeat (rep) Row 141 on odd-numbered rows and Row 142 on even-numbered rows.

Rows 221–240 (20 rows): With Color A, work in garter st.

Row 241: With Color A, knit 20 sts; with Color H, knit 40 sts; with Color I, knit 40 sts; with Color J, knit 40 sts; with Color A, knit 20 sts.

Row 242: With Color A, knit 20 sts; with Color J, knit 40 sts; with Color I, knit 40 sts; with Color H, knit 40 sts; with Color A, knit 20 sts.

Rows 243–320 (78 rows): Repeat Row 241 on odd-numbered rows, and Row 242 on even-numbered rows.

Rows 321–340 (20 rows): With Color A, work in garter st.

Row 341: With Color A, knit 20 sts; with Color K, knit 40 sts; with Color L, knit 40 sts; with Color M, knit 40 sts; with Color A, knit 20 sts.

Row 342: With Color A, knit 20 sts; with Color M, knit 40 sts; with Color L, knit 40 sts; with Color K, knit 40 sts; with Color A, knit 20 sts.

Rows 343–420 (78 rows): Rep Row 341 on odd-numbered rows, and Row 342 on even-numbered rows.

Rows 421–460 (40 rows): With Color A, work in garter st.

Finishing

Bind off (BO) all sts. With a tapestry needle, weave in loose yarn tails to WS of work and secure.

4

for little ones

Need a little **something to knit** for your smaller-sized friends? This chapter has items designed for pals of both the two-legged and the four-legged variety.

The Curlilocks Finger Puppet (page 80) is as much fun for adults to play with as children. Likewise, Knitted Kick Sacks (page 83) are welcomed by kids and stressed-out adults. Make three and improve your juggling skills.

Want to make your cat as crazy as it probably makes you when you knit? With small amounts of yarn, you can make the cat its very own Catnip Friend (page 88), and perhaps your feline friend will leave you and your knitting alone!

The spiral patterning in the Ruffled Baby Tube Socks, Mitts, and Caps (page 84) is easy and fun to knit. I think if you start knitting one, you will want to make a whole set! Because of their diminutive size, they don't require a lot of yarn either.

Don't forget the dog! He or she deserves to look smashing in the multicolored Pampered Pooch Striped Sweater (page 91).

Curlilocks Finger Puppet

Use rustic yarns for a charming homespun look, or pull out all the stops and use your glitzy yarns to make a wardrobe fit for a ball—either way, none of your precious yarns will go to waste.

Finished Size
Height: 4½ inches (11.5 cm)

Yarn
You will need about 1 to 3 yards (91 cm–2.75 m) of assorted colors in a super fine yarn weight, using the same stitch pattern and gauge.

We used Rowan Rowanspun 4 ply (100% pure new wool; 162 yards [148 m]/.88-ounce [25-g] skein). Small amounts of yarn ranging from 1–3 yards (91 cm–2.75 m) of the following colors:
Color A—#727 Lunar
Color B—#721 Ginger Bread
Color C—#726 Hansel
Color F—#724 Siren

Rowan Lightweight DK (100% wool; 74 yards [67 m]/ .88-ounce [25-g] skein). Small amounts of yarn ranging from 1 to 3 yards (91 cm–2.75 m) of the following colors:
Color D—#103 Apricot
Color E—#6 Yellow

Needles
US size 1 (2.25 mm) double-point (dpn), set of 4 or 5

Gauge
9 stitches and 12 rows = 1 inch (2.5 cm) in stockinette stitch (St st). Gauge samples were worked back and forth in stitch pattern. Flat knitting usually has a different gauge than circular knitting, but in these small, stretchy items, the difference isn't significant.

Notions
Tapestry needle; small amount of polyester filling; hairspray; plastic drinking straw

Notes
Because of the project's small size, I suggest the following:
1. When casting on fewer than 15 stitches, work the first row flat before joining the stitches into a circle.

2. Use the yarn tail as the stitch marker at the beginning of each round.

Make the Legs (make 2)
The legs are attached to the lower edge of the skirt front, and the skirt back remains open so you can insert a finger and hold the puppet upright.

With Color A, leaving a 6-inch (15-cm) tail to use as a stitch marker, cast on (CO) 12 stitches (sts).

Row 1: (RS) Knit. After completing the row, join work into a circle, being careful not to twist the sts. Place the yarn tail between first and last sts to identify beginning of round (rnd).

Rnds 1–2: Knit.

Rnd 3: K4, knit 2 together (k2tog) twice, k4—(10 sts).

Rnd 4: With Color B, k4, k2tog, k4—(9 sts).

Rnds 5–6: Knit.

Continue alternating 3 rnds of Color A and 3 rnds of Color B until you have created a leg with 4 stripes of each color, ending with Color B. Cut the yarn, leaving a 6-inch (15-cm) tail. Thread tapestry needle with yarn tail and sew the sts together, keeping the top of the leg flat. Set aside until later.

Make the Skirt and Body
With Color A, CO 32 sts. Join work into a circle, being careful not to twist the sts.

Rnd 1: Purl.

Rnds 2 and 4: *K1 with Color A, k1 with Color B*; repeat (rep) instructions between * * to end of rnd.

Rnd 3: *K1 with Color B, k1 with Color A*; rep instructions between * * to end of rnd.

Rnds 5–8 (4 rnds): With Color B, knit.

Rnds 9–10: (decreases) With Color B, *k2, k2tog*; rep instructions between * * to end of rnd—(18 sts).

Rnd 11: To create the belt, with Color C, knit.

Rnd 12: Purl.

Rnds 13–20 (8 rnds): With Color B, knit.

Rnd 21: To create the neckband, with Color C, knit.

Rnd 22: Purl. Do not bind off (BO).

Make the Head

Rnds 1–2: Leaving a 6-inch (15-cm) tail to use later to form the neck, join Color D and knit both rnds.

Rnd 3: (increases) *K3, knit into the front and back loops of next st (k1f&b)*; rep instructions between * * to last 2 sts, k2 to end rnd—(22 sts).

Rnd 4: (increases) *K3, k1f&b*; rep instructions between * * to last 2 sts, k2 to end rnd—(27 sts).

Rnds 5–10 (6 rnds): Knit.

Rnd 11: (decreases) *K3, k2tog*; rep instructions between * * to last 2 sts, k2 to end rnd—(22 sts).

Rnd 12: (decreases) *K3, k2tog*; rep instructions between * * to last 2 sts, k2 to end rnd—(18 sts).

Rnd 13: (decreases) *K1, k2tog*; rep instructions between * * to end of rnd—(12 sts).

Rnd 14: (decreases) *K2tog; rep from * to end of rnd—(6 sts).

Cut the yarn, leaving a 6-inch (15-cm) tail. Thread tapestry needle with yarn tail and weave through the remaining sts. Pull the yarn tail gently to close the top of the head; weave yarn tail to wrong side (WS) and secure. *Stuff head:* Working from the neck up, stuff the head firmly with polyester filling.

Close Neck

Thread the tapestry needle with the 6-inch (15-cm) yarn tail (Color D) reserved at the base of the head. Weave needle and yarn through the sts around the neck, and then pull the yarn gently to make a slight indentation above the neckband. Thread yarn through several sts to secure, then push into the head to hide the tail.

Facial Features

With Color A threaded on tapestry needle, make two eyes using French knots (see Techniques, page 117). With Color F, make the mouth using small straight embroidery sts.

Make the Arms (make 2)

With Color D, CO 7 sts.

Row 1: Knit. Join work into a circle, being careful not to twist sts.

Rnds 1–2: Knit.

Rnd 3: To form cuff, join Color C, knit.

Rnd 4: Purl.

Rnds 5–9 (5 rnds): With Color B, knit until the arm measures about 1¼ inches (3.2 cm) from the beginning.

Cut the yarn, leaving a 6-inch (15-cm) tail, and thread a tapestry needle. Weave needle and yarn through the sts,

and close the arm tops same as for legs. Leave the CO edge open, and set the arms aside until later.

Make the Hair

Wrap a 60-inch (152.5-cm) strand of Color E yarn tightly around a drinking straw. Spray with hairspray and press the yarn ends onto the straw with your fingertips. When the yarn is completely dry, carefully remove the straw.

Finishing

Legs

Lightly stuff the legs from the foot up with a small amount of the polyester filling, using a knitting needle to help insert the stuffing. Thread tapestry needle with the yarn tail and use to stitch the CO edges together and close the feet. Thread tapestry needle with Color B and sew the legs to the inside front of the skirt, attaching both legs just above the 3 rnds of Fair Isle on the skirt.

Arms

Working from the hands up, lightly stuff the arms with polyester filling as you did for the legs. With Color D, or the CO tail, neatly stitch the hand CO sts to close the lower edge. Thread tapestry needle with Color B yarn and whipstitch the arms to the body just below the neck indentation. Weave in all loose yarn tails to the WS of work and secure.

Attach Hair to Head

Cut two 4-inch (10-cm) strands of yarn, one of Color B and one of Color C. Thread tapestry needle with both strands and sew them to halfway through 1 or 2 sts on the top of the head. The strands should have equal lengths on each side after attaching to the top of the head. Fold the curled hair into quarters and lay the hair flat across the attached strands of Colors B and C. Tie both yarn strands together with overhand knot, securing the hair to the head, and then tie the strands into a bow. Style the hair as desired. Put Curlilocks on your finger and take her dancing!

Knitted Kick Sacks

Otherwise known as footbags, these small sacks are good for kicking around and playing games. They also make colorful paperweights. The directions are given for a striped Knitted Kick Sack, but you can make them in a solid color or your own design.

Finished Size
Height: 2¼ inches (5.5 cm)
Width: 2½ inches (6.5 cm)
Circumference: 8 inches (20.5 cm)

Yarn
You will need about 18 yards (17 m) total (about 2 yards [1.83 m] for each color section) of medium-weight cotton yarn for each stripe, using the same stitch pattern and gauge.

We used Lion Brand Cotton (100% cotton; 236 yards [215 m]/5-ounce [142-g] ball). For each Knitted Kick Sack, you will need about 2 yards (1.83 m) for each color section in the following colors:
Color A—#181 Sage
Color B—#108 Morning Glory Blue
Color C—#186 Maize
Color D—#135 Cinnamon
Color E—#98 Natural

Needles
US size 4 (3.5 mm) double-point (dpn), set of 6.
Adjust the needle size if necessary to obtain the correct gauge.

Gauge
5 stitches and 8 rounds = 1 inch (2.5 cm) in circular stockinette stitch (St st) (knit each round)

Notions
Tapestry needle; dried beans, about 2 ounces (57 g) per Knitted Kick Sack

Note
For this small project, you will be able to identify the beginning of each round by the threads that start it. As you add colors, knot both yarn tails together, and use the yarn tails to help stuff the Knitted Kick Sack.

Make the Knitted Kick Sack

With Color E, cast on 5 stitches (sts). With sts all on one needle, knit into the front and then the back loop of the same st (k1f&b) of each st—(10 sts). Slip each pair of sts onto a new needle—(2 sts on each of 5 needles). Join work into a circle, being careful not to twist sts.

Rnd 1: K1f&b in the first st on each of the 5 needles—(3 sts on each needle, 15 sts total).

Rnd 2: Repeat (rep) Round (Rnd) 1—(4 sts on each needle, 20 sts total).

Rnd 3: Knit all sts, no increases (inc).

Rnds 4–5: Change to Color D and rep Rnd 1—(6 sts on each needle, 30 sts total).

Rnd 6: Join Color A and rep Rnd 1—(7 sts on each needle, 35 sts total).

Rnds 7–16 (10 rnds): Knit all sts without further inc. *At the same time,* while knitting the entire Knitted Kick Sack, change colors of your choosing every 2 rnds.

Rnds 17–20 (4 rnds): Knit 2 together (k2tog) at the beginning of each of the 5 needles—(3 sts on each needle, 15 sts total).

Rnd 21: Knit all sts without decreases (dec).

Rnds 22–23: K2tog at beginning of each needle—(1 st on each needle, 5 sts total).

Finishing

Cut the yarn, leaving a tail about 6 inches (15 cm) long. Thread tapestry needle with yarn tail and weave through the remaining 5 sts. Leave the top open. Fill the Knitted Kick Sack with beans until it is very full. (Make a paper funnel with a large point to use when filling the Knitted Kick Sacks with beans.) Gently pull the tapestry needle and yarn tail to draw the sts together and close the Knitted Kick Sack's top. Weave the tail through several sts on wrong side (WS), then push the tapestry needle to the opposite end of the Knitted Kick Sack, leaving the remaining yarn tail embedded inside.

Bet you can't make just one!

Ruffled Baby Tube Socks, Mitts, and Caps

This classic spiral pattern helps keep the tube socks on a squirming baby. Knit with thicker yarn and bigger needles and increasing the number of stitches around, this basic concept could be expanded to fit older children, too. (For the spiral pattern to work, you need a multiple of 3 stitches plus 1.)

● ● ●

Stash-Busting Tip

Think coordinating, but not necessarily identical. You can apply this principle to many knitted items; hats, mittens, gloves, and pillows are just a few.

Finished Size

Socks
Tube socks are not size-specific. These should fit babies from 3 to 12 months.
Circumference: 5 inches (12.5 cm)
Length: 6½ inches (16.5 cm)

Mittens
About 3 to 12 months
Circumference: 5 inches (12.5 cm)
Length: 4 inches (10 cm)

Caps
Small, 3 to 9 months (Medium, 1–2 years)
Circumference: 17 (21) inches (43 [53.5] cm)
Length from top to brim: 4½ (5½) inches (11.5 [14] cm)

Yarn

You will need about 185 yards (169 m) of fine yarn in each color to make 1 pair of tube socks, 2 hats, and 1 pair of shorter-length socks (about 4 inches [10 cm]) to wear as thumbless mittens using the same pattern stitch and gauge.

We used Nature's Palette fingering-weight wool, hand-dyed with natural dyes (100% merino wool; 185 yards [169 m]/1.75-ounce [50-g] skein). 1 skein each of the following colors:
Spring Grass—NP-122, 185 yards (169 m)
Owl's Clover—NP-106, 185 yards (169 m)

Needles

US size 1 (2.25 mm), double-point (dpn), set of 5, for tube socks, mitts, and smaller-size hat; size 3 (3.25 mm) dpn, set of 5, for larger hat. ***Adjust the needle size if necessary to obtain the correct gauge.***

Gauge

Tube socks, mitts, and smaller-size cap:
13 stitches and 25 rounds = 2 inches (5 cm) in spiral pattern stitch. ***Medium cap:*** 10¼ stitches and 19 rounds = 2 inches in spiral pattern stitch

Notions

US size B/1 (2.25 mm) crochet hook; stitch markers; tapestry needle; about 18 inches (46 cm) smooth waste cotton yarn for provisional (temporary) cast-on

Note

Both caps are worked using the same number of sts. The size difference is accomplished by using larger-size needles to make the larger hat.

Make the Baby Tube Socks

With crochet hook and the smooth waste yarn, chain 12 stitches (sts) to make a provisional (temporary) crochet chain cast-on (CO) (see Techniques, page 115).

Row 1: Join main color (MC) yarn. Using the beginning end of the crochet chain, pick up 8 sts from the crochet chain. Work in rows, back and forth in St st, for 4 rows. Beginning at the knotted end of the waste yarn, pull the end out of the last crochet st and then remove the provisional CO, inserting a dpn into the live sts to create a seamless beginning (see Techniques, page 115).

One dpn holds 8 sts at one end of the 4 rows and a second dpn holds 8 sts at the other end of the 4 rows. Fold the 4 rows in half and then slip 4 sts purlwise (pwise) onto each of 4 dpns—(16 sts). Place a marker (pm) on the needle where the working yarn is attached. From this point on, you'll be working in rounds (rnds), and the marker will identify the beginning of the rnd and *Needle #1*.

Next 5 Rnds: Increase (inc) 1 st in the first st at the beginning of each of the 4 needles until there are 9 sts on each needle—(36 sts total).

Begin the Spiral Pattern

Beginning with Needle #1: K2, knit into the front and then the back loop of the next st (k1f&b), p3, *k3, p3; repeat (rep) from *. There is no distinct end of rnd; the pattern (patt) shifts by 1 stitch to the right while working the k3, p3 patt continuously on 37 sts. Work even until the sock measures about 6 inches (15 cm) from the toe beginning.

Make the Contrast Color Ruffle

Cut MC, leaving a 4-inch (10-cm) tail. Join contrast color (CC), knit 1 rnd.

Next rnd: Work in k1, p1 ribbing, ending rnd with k1f&b— (38 sts). Work two more rnds of ribbing.

Finishing

Picot Edge: Bind off (BO) 2 sts, *slip remaining st from right-hand needle to left-hand needle, CO 2 sts, BO 4 sts; rep from * to the end of the round and fasten off remaining st. With a tapestry needle, weave in loose yarn tails to the wrong side (WS) of work and secure.

Rep the above instructions from beginning to make the second sock, reversing the colors as shown in photo (see page 85).

Make the Mitts

Make the mitts using the same directions as for the tube socks until work measures about 3½ inches (9 cm) from beginning. Follow the same instructions to make the ruffle and Picot Edge, changing colors in trim as desired.

Crochet Cord

Measure baby from one wrist to the other, working along the arms and across the back. With crochet hook and yarn color of your choice, make a crochet chain about 2 inches (5 cm) longer than the total measurement. With threaded tapestry needle, attach one end of the cord to each mitt. *Caution:* Mitt and hat cords can be dangerous if baby becomes entangled in them. Make sure the mitt cord is threaded up the jacket sleeve, across the back, and down the other sleeve. One mitt dangles at the end of each sleeve. When the jacket is worn, the cord must be across the baby's back and *not* across the chest or front of neck.

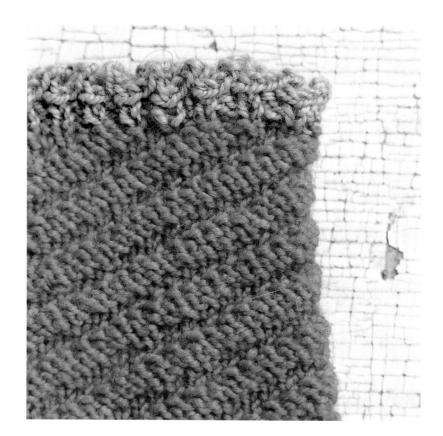

Make the Baby Cap

With CC, work the hat the same as the tube socks through Row 4. Remove waste yarn from provisional CO and, keeping the work flat (don't fold in half), slip 4 sts on each of 4 needles. Place marker before the stitch with the working yarn attached. From this point on you'll be working in rnds, and the marker will identify the beginning of the rnd and Needle #1.

Crown Increases
Rnd 1:

Needle #1: With CC, *slip (sl) 1, k1f&b, k2;

Needle #2: K1f&b, k2, sl 1;

Needle #3: Rep Needle #1;

Needle #4: Rep Needle #2—(20 sts total).

Rnds 2–8 (7 rnds): With CC, *k1, k1f&b, knit to end of needle; repeat from * on each needle—(48 sts total).

Rnds 9–23 (15 rnds): With MC, *k1, k1f&b, knit to end of needle; repeat from * on each needle—(27 sts on each needle, 108 sts total).

Begin the Spiral Pattern

Beginning with Needle #1: K2, k1f&b, p3, *k3, p3; rep from * working continuously in a spiral and ignoring the end-of-rnd marker. The spiral pattern moves to the right by 1 stitch while working the k3, p3 patt over 109 sts. Work even until hat measures 3¾ (5) inches (9.5 [12.5] cm).

Make the Edging

Small-size cap only: Cut MC, leaving a 4-inch (10-cm) tail. Join CC, knit 1 rnd. *Next rnd:* Work in k1, p1 ribbing to last st, k1f&b—(110 sts). Work 4 more rnds of ribbing. Begin Picot Edge.

Medium-size cap only: Continue with MC and work in k1, p1 ribbing to last st, k1f&b—(110 sts). Work 6 more rnds of ribbing. Cut MC, leaving a 4-inch (10-cm) tail. Join CC and begin Picot Edge.

Finishing

Picot Edge: BO 2 sts, *slip remaining st on right-hand needle onto left-hand needle, CO 2 sts, BO 4 sts; rep from * to the end of the round and fasten off remaining st. With tapestry needle, weave in loose yarn tails to wrong side of work and secure.

Hand-wash all items and allow to air-dry before wearing.

Catnip Friends

Make a mouse for the felines that live in your house, or give a mouse or two to your devoted cat friends. The mice take very little yarn to make and are quick to knit. Of course, you can fill one of these little friends with lavender or other fresh herbs and use them yourself!

Finished Size
About 2¼ inches (5.5 cm) wide, 5 inches (12.5 cm) long (excluding tail)

Yarn
You will need about 23 yards (21 m) total of medium-weight yarn, using the same stitch pattern and gauge.

For the gray and black nubby-textured mouse, we used Artful Yarns Legend (83% wool, 17% nylon; 78 yards [71 m]/1.75-ounce [50-g] ball): #1493 Blackbeard, 23 yards (21 m)

For the gray mouse, we used Rowan Rowanspun Chunky (100% pure new wool; 142 yards [130 m]/ 3.5-ounce [100-g] skein): #984 Silver, 23 yards (21 m)

Needles
US size 6 (4 mm) double-point (dpn), set of 4

Gauge
Because these mice don't have to fit, the gauge is not critical, but the fabric you create must be dense or the catnip will fall out.

Notions
Tapestry needle; markers; catnip; sewing needle; embroidery thread to attach beads and make whiskers; 3 small beads for the eyes and nose; small bell for end of tail, if desired

Note
Firmly sew beads onto the mouse because they can be dangerous if ingested.

Make the Mouse

Using dpns, cast on (CO) 21 stitches (sts), leaving a yarn tail that will be used later to create the mouse's tail. Place marker and join into a circle, being careful not to twist sts. Work in circ stockinette stitch (St st) (knit all rounds) until piece measures 2½ inches (6.5 cm).

Shape Nose
Next round (rnd): Using the knit 2 sts together method (k2tog), decrease (dec) a total of 3 sts evenly spaced—(18 sts remain). Knit 2 rnds. Repeat (rep) these last three rnds until 6 sts remain. K2tog 3 times—(3 sts remain). Cut yarn and thread tail through remaining 3 sts.

Ears (make 2)
CO 2 sts. Knit next row and increase (inc) 1 st using the make 1 (M1) method (see Abbreviations, page 120). Purl 1 row. Knit 1 row. Purl 1 row. BO 3 sts.

Finishing

Sew the ears to mouse and, *at the same time,* using a running stitch, sew the ends of the yarn around the edges of the ears to give them a curvy mouse-ear shape. Using the yarn or embroidery thread, attach the beads to form the eyes and nose (see photo). If desired, add whiskers with the embroidery floss or yarn.

Stuff the mouse with catnip. With tapestry needle, thread about 12 inches (30.5 cm) yarn through the end of the mouse and draw the end together to seal in the stuffing.

Tail: Thread a tapestry needle with a 28-inch (71-cm) strand of yarn and sew through 1 st next to the 12-inch (30.5-cm) yarn tail. Pull the strand through to the halfway point. You will have two 14-inch (35.5-cm) strands plus the 12-inch (30.5-cm) strand grouped together at the tail end of the mouse. Braid the 3 strands together to the desired tail length. Tie a knot in end of tail and trim ends to even. Attach a small bell with sewing thread or yarn, if desired.

Pampered Pooch Striped Sweater

Many of us have on hand a variety of medium-weight yarns that lend themselves to myriad fun projects, like this dog sweater. To pull the different colors together, I used dark blue for the collar, cuffs, and ribbed trim.

Finished Size
(This sweater fits a dog about the size of a cocker spaniel, about 20 pounds.)
Length: About 16 inches (40.5 cm)
Neck circumference: 16 inches (40.5 cm), unstretched
Chest circumference: 26 inches (66 cm)

Yarn
You will need about 274 yards (250 m) total of medium-weight yarn, using the same stitch pattern and gauge. This dog sweater can be made using a wide variety of yarns. Vary the width of the color bands to accommodate the amounts of stash yarns suitable for the project.

We used Black Water Abbey Yarn (2-ply worsted weight 100% new wool; 220 yards [201 m]/4-ounce [113-g] skein).

Color A—Dark Slate, 100 yards (91 m)
Color B—Rust, 6 yards (5 m)
Color C—Butter, 6 yards (5 m)
Color D—Moss, 7 yards (6.4 m)
Color E—Autumn, 7 yards (6.4 m)
Color F—Bluestack, 7 yards (6.4 m)
Color G—Wheat, 8 yards (7.3 m)
Color H—Pink Heather, 8 yards (7.3 m)
Color I—Ocean, 25 yards (23 m)
Color J—Wine, 25 yards (23 m)
Color K—Bracken, 25 yards (23 m)
Color L—Iris, 25 yards (23 m)
Color M—Jacob, 25 yards (23 m)

Needles
US size 6 (4 mm) circular (circ) 16-inch (40-cm); US size 8 (5 mm) circ 24-inch (61-cm); US size 8 (5 mm) pair of straight needles, or a second circ needle same size; US size 6 (4 mm) double-point needles (dpn), set of 4 or 5, for leg cuffs. **Adjust the needle size if necessary to obtain the correct gauge.**

Gauge
17 stitches and 27 rows = 4 inches (10 cm) in stockinette stitch (St st) on larger-size needles

Notions
US size H/8 (5 mm) crochet hook; 2 or 3 yards (1.8–2.7 m) smooth waste cotton yarn for provisional (temporary) cast-on; markers; stitch holder; tapestry needle; long straight sewing pins with large colored heads

Note
Continue making 12-row or 12-rnd stripes using the color sequence in alphabetical order as you complete the rest of the sweater.

Make the Neck

With crochet hook and smooth waste yarn, chain about 95 stitches (sts) to make a provisional (temporary) crochet chain cast-on (CO) (see Techniques, page 115). Cut the waste yarn, leaving a 4-inch (10-cm) tail, thread through the end of the last loop, and pull to secure. Tie a knot in the tail of the yarn to help you identify this end later when you need to remove the chain. With Color A and smaller-size circ needle, knit 1 st in each of 84 consecutive chain bumps—(84 sts). Place a marker (pm) to mark the beginning of the round (rnd) and join work into a circle, being careful not to twist the sts.

Neckband
Work in rnds of k1, p1 ribbing until the neckband measures 1½ inches (11.5 cm) from the beginning. Purl one rnd to make a turning ridge and return to k1, p1 ribbing for another 1½ inches (11.5 cm).

Make the Yoke

Switch to larger-size needles.

Rnds 1–3 (3 rnds): With Color A, knit.

Rnd 4: Purl.

Rnd 5: With Color B, knit 1 rnd.

Rnd 6: (increases) Knit, increasing (inc) 4 sts evenly spaced as follows: *K21, make 1; repeat (rep) from * to end of rnd—(88 sts).

Rnd 7: Knit.

Rnd 8: Purl.

Rnd 9: With Color C, knit.

Rnd 10: (increases) Knit, inc 4 sts evenly spaced as follows: *k22, m1 (see Abbreviations, page 120); rep from * to end of rnd—(92 sts).

Rnds 11–12: Rep Rnds 7 and 8.

Rnd 13: With Color D, knit.

Rnd 14: (increases) Knit, inc 4 sts evenly spaced as follows: *k23, m1; rep from * to end of rnd—(96 sts).

Rnds 15–16: Repeat Rnds 7 and 8.

Rnd 17: With Color E, knit.

Rnd 18: (increases) Knit, inc 4 sts evenly spaced as follows: *k24, m1; rep from * to end of rnd—(100 sts).

Rnds 19–20: Rep Rnds 7 and 8.

Rnd 21: With Color F, knit.

Rnd 22: (increases) Knit, inc 12 sts evenly spaced as follows: k10, m1, [k8, m1] 10 times, k10, m1—(112 sts).

Rnd 23: Knit.

Rnd 24: Purl.

Rnd 25: With Color G, knit.

Rnd 26: (increases) Knit, inc 12 sts evenly spaced as follows: k11, m1, [k9, m1] 10 times, k11, m1—(124 sts).

Rnds 27–28: Rep Rnds 7 and 8.

Rnds 29–31 (3 rnds): With Color H, knit.

Rnd 32: Purl.

Rnds 33–44 (12 rnds): With Color I, knit. *At the same time,* when work measures 5½ inches (14 cm) from the beginning of the yoke, begin leg openings.

Make the Leg Openings

Underpanel

Beginning at the marker, with straight needles (or use a second circ needle of same size) knit across 15 sts. Turn work to wrong side (WS) and purl back across these 15 sts plus 15 sts on the other side of the marker for a total of 30 sts. Leave the remaining 94 sts on a circular needle. These 94 sts are reserved for the back. Work back and forth in rows of St st on the 30 underpanel sts for 3¼ inches (8.5 cm), ending with a WS row.

Cut yarn, and with right side (RS) facing, attach the correct color yarn to beginning of reserved back sts and work flat back and forth on these 94 sts until this piece measures the same length as the underpanel, ending with a WS row. Having created two slits for the leg openings, the work resumes as circ knitting in the round as follows: Join the correct color yarn at a marker between underpanel sts. Maintaining the striped pattern, with RS facing, begin at the marker and k15 of the 30 underpanel sts, then k94 back sts, then k15 (last 15 sts of underpanel); join work into rnd at marker. Work even in rnds and stripes until the sweater measures 10 inches (25.5 cm) from the beginning of the yoke.

To Form the Shaped Back Edge

Place the 30 underpanel sts on a st holder, with stitch marker in place. Keep the remaining 94 back sts on the circ needle, join yarn, and work flat back and forth on these sts, binding off 1 st at the beginning of each row for 20 rows—(74 sts). Cut yarn, leaving a 4-inch (10-cm) tail.

Make the Ribbed Border

With RS of work facing, place the 30 underpanel sts on the 24-inch (60-cm) smaller-size circ needle. Join Color A at marker (halfway between the 30 sts), begin at marker, k15 sts, pick up and k24 sts along shaped side edge, k74 sts across sweater back, then pick up and k24 sts along remaining shaped side edge, then knit the remaining 15 underpanel sts—(152 sts). Work in rnds of k1, p1 ribbing until border measures about 1 inch (2.3 cm). Bind off (BO) all sts.

Make the Leg Cuffs

With Color A and dpns, pick up 38 sts around the edge of the leg slit and work in k1, p1 ribbing until cuff measures ¾ inch (2 cm). BO. With a tapestry needle, weave in loose yarn tails to the WS and secure. Work second cuff in same manner.

Finishing

Remove provisional crochet chain CO at neck, placing live sts on circ needle to hold. Fold neckband at purl ridge to WS of work. Pin the neckband in place. Thread tapestry needle with Color A, and weave 1 live st from the circ needle to a corresponding st from the first body row. Don't pull sewing yarn too tightly; try to maintain the same elasticity as the rest of the neckband so it will easily stretch over poochie's head. Remove pins. With a tapestry needle, weave in loose yarn tails to WS of work and secure.

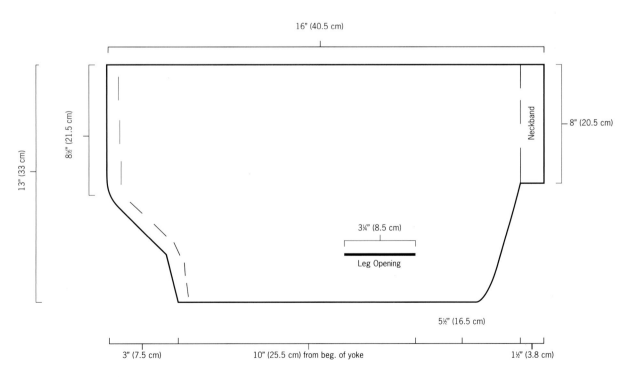

16" (40.5 cm)

8½" (21.5 cm)

13" (33 cm)

Neckband

8" (20.5 cm)

3¼" (8.5 cm)

Leg Opening

5½" (16.5 cm)

3" (7.5 cm)

10" (25.5 cm) from beg. of yoke

1½" (3.8 cm)

⑤

for scarf lovers

Sometimes you find an irresistible yarn that you just *have* to own and knit with. Scarves are often the perfect project for these splurges. If your basic black or denim look is getting tiresome, a wonderful scarf could be just what the fashion doctor ordered. With the seemingly limitless choices of colors, textures, fibers, and stitch patterns, there's a good reason why some stashes become so large and why some knitters never move beyond making scarves.

While garter stitch, seed stitch, ribbing, and basketweave are all great stitch patterns to use when making scarves, the inspired stitch patterns and styles herein will make terrific additions to your scarf repertoire. Included are a couple of my favorites and a few great designs from my knitting buddies.

Make sure to check out stitch pattern books for inspiration. Using the same stitch pattern with a variety of yarns and needle sizes can create many looks. Scarves are a great place to try out intriguing stitch patterns as well as to sample interesting yarns.

Keep in mind that the edges of stockinette stitch tend to curl. A few garter stitches or seed stitches along the edges of the scarf and a few rows of garter stitch or seed stitch at the ends of the scarf can help keep the fabric flat and under control, as shown in the examples. Another option is to add a row of single crochet or another crochet stitch as a border for the outside edges of the scarf.

Sumptuously Soft Scarf

Designer Linda Romens fell in love with this fabulous berry-colored qiviut yarn and just had to have it. Qiviut, which comes from the Arctic musk ox, is one of the warmest, softest natural fibers known to man. This scarf design would be beautiful made in other luxury fibers such as cashmere or yak down.

Finished Size
Width: 6 inches (15 cm)
Length: 68 inches (173 cm)

Yarn
You will need about 275 yards (251 m) total of light-weight yarn using the same stitch pattern and gauge.

We used Mini-Mills 3-ply qiviut (275 yards [251 m]/ 2-ounce [57-g] skein:
Burgundy, 1 skein

Needles
US size 6 (4 mm). *Adjust the needle size if necessary to obtain the correct gauge.*

Gauge
18 stitches and 24 rows = 4 inches (10 cm) in pattern stitch

Notions
Tapestry needle

Note
We have given both the text and chart instructions for this scarf. See ssk details in Abbreviations, page 120.

Pattern Stitch

Row 1 and all other wrong side (WS) rows: K5, p17, k5.
Row 2: K4, p1, k5, yarn over (yo), slip, slip knit decrease (ssk), k2, knit 2 stitches (sts) together (k2tog), yo, k1, yo, ssk, k3, p1, k4.

Row 4: K4, p1, k3, k2tog, yo, k1, yo, ssk, (k2tog, yo) twice, k1, yo, ssk, k2, p1, k4.

Row 6: K4, p1, k2, (k2tog, yo) twice, k1, yo, ssk, k2tog, yo, k1, (yo, ssk) twice, k1, p1, k4.

Row 8: K4, p1, k1, (k2tog, yo) twice, k3, yo, ssk, yo, work a double decrease (dec) as follows: ssk, then return the remaining ssk st to the left needle, pass the next st on the left needle over the ssk st, and slip (sl) the ssk st back to the right needle and continue the row, yo, k2tog, yo, k2, p1, k4.

Row 10: K4, p1, (k2tog, yo) twice, k5, yo, ssk, k1, k2tog, yo, k3, p1, k4.

Row 12: K4, p1, k1, k2tog, yo, k2, yo, ssk, k3, yo, ssk and pass next st, yo, k4, p1, k4.

Row 14: K4, p1, k3, k2tog, yo, k1, yo, ssk, k2, k2tog, yo, k5, p1, k4.

Row 16: K4, p1, k2, k2tog, yo, k1, (yo, ssk) twice, k2tog, yo, k1, yo, ssk, k3, p1, k4.

Row 18: K4, p1, k1, (k2tog, yo) twice, k1, yo, ssk, k2tog, yo, k1, (yo, ssk) twice, k2, p1, k4.

Row 20: K4, p1, k2, yo, ssk, yo, sl 1, k2tog, pass slipped stitch over (psso), yo, k2tog, yo, k3, (yo, ssk) twice, k1, p1, k4.

Row 22: K4, p1, k3, yo, ssk, k1, k2tog, yo, k5, (yo, ssk) twice, p1, k4.

Row 24: K4, p1, k4, yo, sl 1, k2tog, psso, yo, k3, k2tog, yo, k2, yo, ssk, k1, p1, k4.

Make the Scarf

Cast on (CO) 27 sts. Knit 6 rows (not shown on chart).

Next row: Follow the chart or begin with Row 1 of text instructions for the pattern stitch. Repeat Rows 1–24 until the scarf measures about 1 inch (2.5 cm) from finished length, ending with Row 24. Work Row 1 once more. Knit 7 rows. Bind off (BO).

Finishing

With a tapestry needle, weave in loose yarn tails to WS of work and secure. Block the scarf, stretching the lace pattern to display the openwork.

Key

☐ Knit on RS; purl on WS

• Purl on RS; knit on WS

◣ Ssk (see Abbreviations, page 120)

◢ K2tog (see Abbreviations, page 120)

Ⓞ Yarn over

◤ Ssk, return st to left needle, pass the next st over the ssk st, sl the st to the right needle, then proceed with next st.

⅄ Sl 1, k2tog, psso (see Abbreviations, page 120)

☐ Repeat pattern frame

Chart rows (right side): 24, 22, 20, 18, 16, 14, 12, 10, 8, 6, 4, 2

Chart rows (left side): 23, 21, 19, 17, 15, 13, 11, 9, 7, 5, 3, 1

Begin with Row 1 (WS of work), following chart from left to right.

Work Row 2 (RS of work), following chart from right to left.

Continue working chart through Row 24. Repeat Rows 1–24 until scarf measures about 1inch (2.5 cm) from finished length. Finish with Row 24, then work Row 1. Follow text instructions to complete.

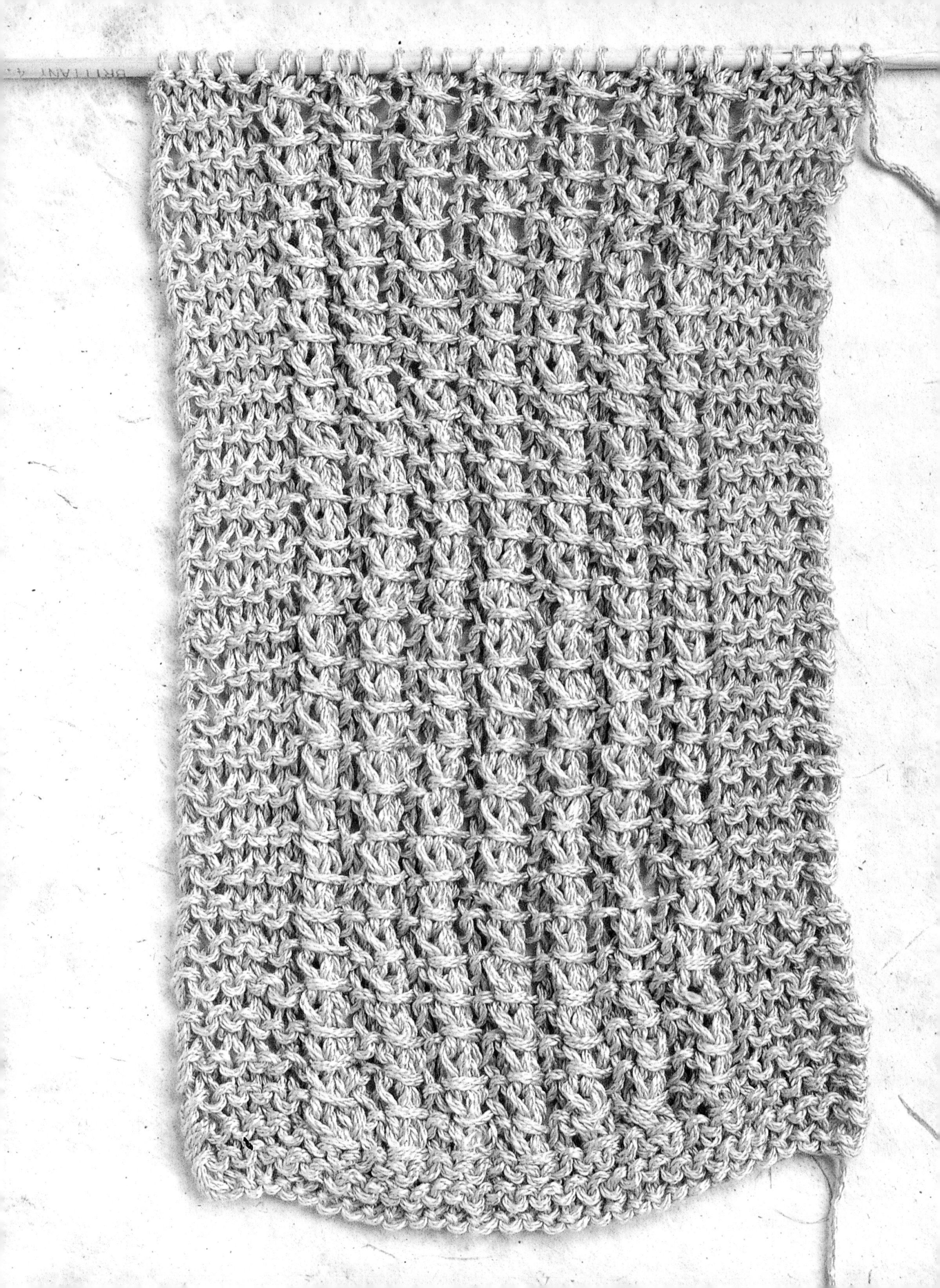

Silk Bamboo Ribbed Scarf

The knitting entrepreneur behind www.knitkit.com, Janet Scanlon, selected this silk from her stash to design this appealing scarf. Framed in garter stitch, bamboo ribs create texture to capture the light as it dances on the silk.

Finished Size
Width: 5 inches (13 cm)
Length: 48 inches (122 cm)

Yarn
You will need about 300 yards (274 m) total of medium-weight yarn to make a scarf in the same stitch pattern and gauge. Although silk is special, many lustrous yarns work equally well. A longer scarf will require more yarn.

We used Treenway Silks (60/2, 100% Bombyx silk; 325 yards [297 m]/3.5-ounce [100-g] skein): #53 Wild Orchid, about 300 yards (274 m)

Needles
US size 7 (4.5 mm). *Adjust the needle size if necessary to obtain the correct gauge.*

Gauge
24 stitches and 24 rows = 4 inches (10 cm) in bamboo rib pattern

Notions
Tapestry needle; 2 stitch markers to mark between the borders and main pattern stitch

Bamboo Rib Stitch Pattern
(multiple of 3 stitches)

Row 1: [K1, bring the yarn forward and over the needle (yo), k2, pass the yo over the k2]; repeat (rep) instructions between [ ] as necessary.

Row 2: [P2, k1]; rep instructions between [ ] as necessary.

Rep these 2 rows for pattern.

Make the Scarf

Cast on (CO) 30 sts.

Rows 1–3: Knit.

Row 4: (RS) K5, place a marker (pm), [yo, k2, pass the yo over the k2, k1] 6 times, yo, k2, pass the yarn over the k2, pm, k5.

Row 5: (WS) K5, slip marker, [p2, k1] 6 times, p2, slip marker, k5.

Rep Rows 4 and 5 until the scarf measures 47 inches (119 cm) from CO edge. End after completing a wrong side (WS) row.

Knit 3 rows. Bind off (BO) kwise (as if to knit) on WS row.

Finishing

With a tapestry needle, weave in loose yarn tails along the side edges and secure. When finished, make a few tugs along the scarf to set the stitches, or hand-wash and block to size.

Easy Side-to-Side Garter Scarf

Instead of knitting a scarf from one short end to the other, this scarf is knit lengthwise from side to side. Made with merino wool and kid mohair, the scarf shown here is luxuriously soft and comfy against the neck. If you plan to add a fringe—which is a good way to use up extra yarn—you can leave yarn tails, the same length as your planned fringe strands, at the beginning and end of each row, and later work them into the main fringe. You'll eliminate the need to weave in yarn tails.

Finished Size
Width: 6½ inches (16.5 cm)
Length: 60 inches (152.5 cm)

Yarn
You will need about 325 yards (297 m) total of medium-weight yarn used as single strand and about 125 yards (114 m) of fine yarn worked with 2 strands together to create a scarf without fringe using the same stitch pattern and gauge.

We used Mostly Merino 2-ply worsted-weight merino (77% wool, 23% mohair; 125 yards [114 m]/2-ounce [57-g] skein):
Color A—Loden, 125 yards (114 m)
Color B—Moss, 125 yards (114 m)

Brooks Farm Fiber hand-dyed mohair (100% kid mohair yarn; 500 yards [457 m]/8-ounce [227-g] skein):
Color C—Primero, 125 yards (114 m). This yarn is worked with 2 strands held together as one.

Needles
US size 8 (5 mm) circular (circ), either 29-inch (73.5-cm) or 32-inch (81.5-cm) length. The scarf is worked back and forth in rows. However, a circular needle is recommended to accommodate all the stitches. *Adjust the needle size if necessary to obtain the correct gauge.*

Gauge
16 stitches and 32 rows = 4 inches (10 cm) in garter stitch

Notions
Tapestry needle

Note
Use this scarf concept with any size needles and appropriate yarn. Make a swatch, measure it, then plan accordingly to make the desired length.

Make the Scarf

With Color A, cast on (CO) 240 stitches (sts). Knit 4 rows.

With Color C, using 2 strands held together, knit 4 rows.

With Color B, knit 4 rows.

With Color C, using 2 strands held together, knit 4 rows.

With Color B, knit 4 rows.

With Color C, using 2 strands held together, knit 4 rows.

With Color A, knit 4 rows.

With Color C, using 2 strands held together, knit 4 rows.

With Color B, knit 4 rows.

With Color C, using 2 strands held together, knit 4 rows.

With Color B, knit 4 rows.

With Color C, using 2 strands held together, knit 4 rows.

With Color A, knit 4 rows.

Bind off (BO).

Finishing

Without Fringe: With a tapestry needle, weave in loose yarn tails to wrong side (WS) of work and secure.

With Fringe: If you began and ended each row by leaving long yarn tails to use for fringing, fill in the fringing by cutting strands twice the length of the current yarn tail. Use 2 strands per color. Fold strands in half and pull through row edges using crochet hook. Fold ends through the halfway loop (including yarn tail) and pull to tighten. If you have extra yarn left over, cut more strands to make a thicker fringe.

Buttons and Stripes Ribbed Scarf

Leslie Ferrero, who designed this scarf, uses a rich neutral shade of brown to tie together sophisticated autumnal shades of yarn. Antique brass buttons from Leslie's button stash make a delightful addition to the end of the scarf. Think about using your own button collection to trim the ends of a scarf!

Finished Size
Width: 6½ inches (16.5 cm)
Length: 60 inches (152.5 cm)

Yarn
You will need about 480 yards (439 m) total of fine-weight yarn using the same stitch pattern and gauge.

We used Blue Sky Alpacas (100% alpaca; 120 yards [110 m]/2-ounce [57-g] ball):
Color A—#001 Natural Dark Brown, 120 yards (110 m)
Color B—#23 Red, 90 yards (82 m)
Color C—#73 Tarnished Gold, 90 yards (82 m)
Color D—#002 Natural Copper, 90 yards (82 m)
Color E—#211 Paprika, 90 yards (82 m)

Needles
US size 4 (3.5 mm). *Adjust the needle size if necessary to obtain the correct gauge.*

Gauge
20 stitches and 24 rows = 4 inches (10 cm) in stockinette stitch

Notions
Tapestry needle; 8 buttons; sewing needle and thread if the holes in the buttons are too small to sew with yarn

Note
When changing colors, drop the current color and pick up the new color from beneath the current one to avoid creating a gap between colors.

Make the Scarf

Cast on (CO) 43 stitches (sts) in Color A.

Row 1: (RS) With Color A, *p3, k7; repeat (rep) from * 3 more times—(40 sts), end row with p3.

Row 2: (WS) With Color A, *k3, p7; rep from * 3 more times, end row with k3.

Work Rows 1 and 2 for 6 rows. Piece should measure about 1 inch (2.5 cm) from CO edges. End after finishing a Row 2.

Begin Intarsia Stripe Pattern
Divide Color A onto 5 bobbins, and work Color A from separate bobbins across the row; do not strand the yarn across the other colors. Work the other 4 colors directly from each yarn ball, or wind each color onto its own bobbin.

Row 7: (RS) With first bobbin of Color A, p3;

with Color B, k7;

with second bobbin of Color A, p3;

with Color C, k7;

with third bobbin of Color A, p3;

with Color D, k7;

with fourth bobbin of Color A, p3;

with Color E, k7;

with fifth bobbin of Color A, p3.

Row 8: (WS) With Color A, k3;

with Color E, p7;

with Color A, k3;

with Color D, p7;

with Color A, k3;

with Color C, p7;

with Color A, k3;

with Color B, p7;

with Color A, k3.

Rep Rows 7 and 8 until scarf measures about 58 inches (147.5 cm), or 1 inch (2.5 cm) less than desired length. End after completing a WS row.

End Border
Using Color A only, work Rows 1 and 2 for 6 rows or 1 inch (2.5 cm). Bind off (BO) all sts.

Finishing

With a tapestry needle, weave loose yarn tails into side edges and to the wrong side (WS) of work and secure. *Optional:* With threaded needle, attach 1 button on right side (RS) of work and centered on each k7 section across both end borders worked in Color A—(8 buttons total).

Herringbone Scarf with Moorish Tassels

Fiber friend, designer, and owner of Hand Jive Knits, Darlene Hayes designed this carefully thought out scarf pattern using merino yarn from her line of naturally dyed yarns, Nature's Palette. This scarf would be equally at home over a turtleneck with jeans or worn to add interest to a business suit.

Finished Size
Width: 7¼ inches (18.5 cm)
Length: 62 inches (157.5 cm)

Yarn
You will need about 500 yards (457 m) of fine-weight yarn using the same stitch pattern and gauge. 8 inches (20.5 cm) worked in scarf pattern used 60 yards (55 m)/17 g. 5 tassels used 21 yards (19 m)/6 g.

We used Nature's Palette Fingering weight (100% merino wool; 185 yards [169 m]/1.75-ounce [50-g] skein):
NP-122 Spring Grass, 500 yards (457 m)

Needles
US size 5 (3.75 mm). *Adjust the needle size if necessary to obtain the correct gauge.*

Gauge
29 stitches and 40 rows = 4 inches (10 cm) in pattern stitch

Notions
Tapestry needle

Herringbone Pattern

Row 1: (RS) K1, *k1, p2, k2, p2, k1, p2, k2, p2, k2; repeat (rep) from * once.

Row 2: *P1, k2, p2, k2, p3, k2, p2, k2; rep from * once, p1.

Row 3: K1, *p1, k2, p2, k5, p2, k2, p1, k1; rep from * once.

Row 4: *P3, k2, p2, k1, p1, k1, p2, k2, p2; rep from * once, p1.

Make the Scarf

Cast on (CO) 33 stitches (sts) loosely. Work in herringbone pattern until length desired. Bind off.

Make 10 Moorish tassels (instructions follow) and attach them to both ends of the scarf at the outer edges and at each column of knitted sts.

Finishing

With a tapestry needle, weave in loose yarn tails along the side edges and secure.

Make the Moorish Tassels

Cut a piece of cardboard about 3 inches (7.5 cm) on one side. Fix one end of your yarn to one edge of the cardboard with a piece of masking tape, then wrap the yarn around the cardboard for 20 wraps. Cut the yarn at the end of the last wrap.

Next, take a 16-inch (40.5-cm) strand of the yarn and fold it in half. We'll call this the *attachment yarn* because it's used later to attach the tassel to the scarf. Slide the folded end of the attachment yarn under the loops of yarn on the cardboard, and place it at one end. Pass the loose ends of the attachment yarn through the folded end, then pull the loose ends tight so the yarn on the cardboard is gathered into a firm bunch, making the top of the tassel. Cut the bottom loops of yarn to free the tassel, and remove the masking tape.

Take another piece of yarn, about 18 inches (46 cm) long, and tie a knot in one end for identification. Lay this piece of yarn on top of the tassel with the knot down near the cut ends. Loop it back on itself so that you have a loop of yarn near the top of the tassel. Keeping the loop, use the long end to wrap around the top end of the tassel, about 10 to 12 times, forming a nice, tight head. Slip the remainder through the loop, then pull on the end with the knot until the loop, and the yarn that was passed through it, disappears underneath the wraps. Trim ends to even up, if necessary.

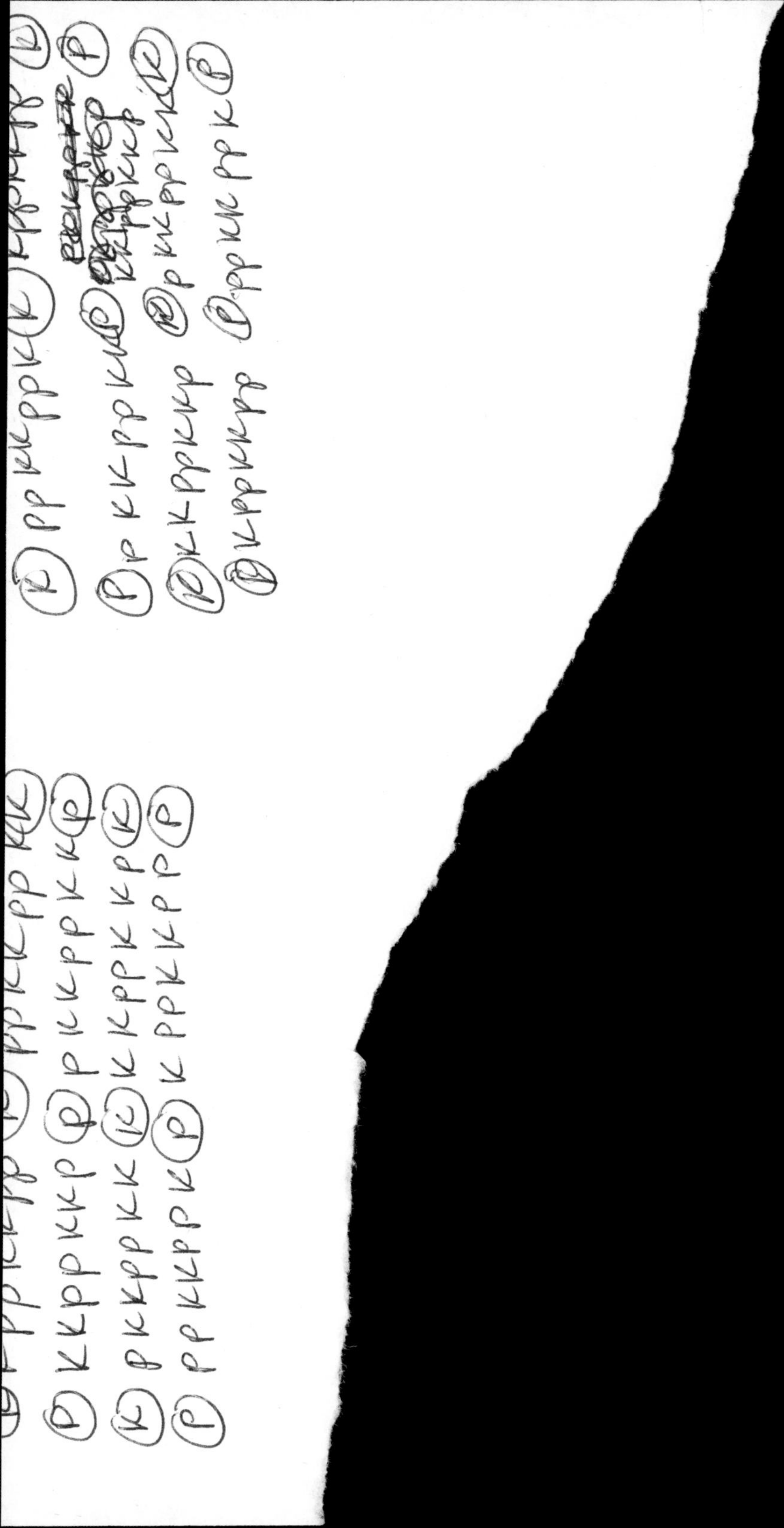

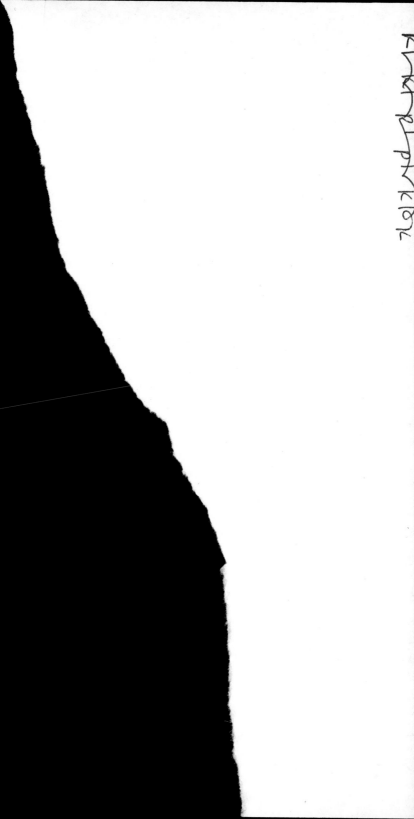

Classic Rugby Stripe Scarf

Jennifer Lindsay has been making many variations of this classic scarf to give as gifts to men, women, teens, and children because it's so easy to personalize. The scarf is knitted in the round on 16-inch circular needles and forms a long tube. Its clean, tailored look comes from the slipped stitches at the side edges on every other row, which set crisp folds in the double-thick fabric so it lies flat when worn.

Finished Size
Width: 6¾ inches (17 cm)
Length: 52 inches (132 cm)

Yarn
You will need about 525 yards (480 m) total of fine-weight yarn to make a 52-inch (132-cm) scarf, using the same stitch pattern and gauge. For a longer scarf, each stripe takes about 25 yards (23 m), and each stripe measures 2½ inches (6.5 cm), so check your stash and calculate what you need.

We used Jaeger Yarns Extra Fine Merino DK (100% Merino wool; 137 yards [125 m]/1.75-ounce [50-g] skein):
Color A—#944 Elderberry, 2 skeins
Color B—#920 Wineberry, 2 skeins
Color C—#923 Satinwood, 2 skeins

Needles
US size 5 (3.75 mm) 16-inch (40.5-cm) circular (circ).
Adjust the needle size if necessary to obtain the correct gauge.

Gauge
22 stitches and 32 rows = 4 inches (10 cm) in circular stockinette stitch

Notions
Tapestry needle

Note
You can make this scarf in bulkier yarns by using fewer stitches (for example, 15–32–15 sts), but Jennifer doesn't recommend yarns much bulkier than 4½ to 5 stitches to the inch (2.5 cm), as the scarf is doubled in thickness.

Make the Scarf

With Color A, cast on (CO) 74 stitches (sts). K18, place marker (to mark side fold), k38, place marker (to mark side fold), k18, place marker (to mark start of new round). Join work into a circle, being careful not to twist sts.

Rnd 1: Knit.

Rnd 2: K18, slip marker (sl m), sl 1 st, k36, sl 1, sl m, k18, sl m.

Repeat (rep) Rnds 1 and 2 using Color A for a total of 20 rnds. Change to Color B and rep Rnds 1 and 2 for 20 rnds. Change to Color C and rep Rnds 1 and 2 for 20 rnds. Rep the instructions between * * 2 more times for a total of 9 stripes. To make the right and left sides of the scarf match when it is worn, do an *around-the-neck* sequence as follows: 20 rnds Color A, 20 rnds Color B, 20 rnds Color A. Now reverse the order of the 9 stripes preceding the neck sequence so they match each other from the neck down, as follows: *20 rnds Color C, 20 rnds Color B, and 20 rnds Color A*; rep from * to * until you have completed the 9 stripes for the left side. Knit 1 additional rnd at the end of the last stripe (21 rnds), and then bind off (BO) all stitches.

Finishing

Turn scarf inside out. With a tapestry needle, weave in loose yarn tails to wrong side (WS) of work and secure. Turn scarf right side out again, and flatten it so the slip stitch folds crease at the side edges and the jog that marks the beginning of the rounds runs up the center back of the scarf. Using a tapestry needle and leftover yarn, sew up the openings at each end of the tube so the scarf lies flat. Block or steam lightly.

Design © 2004 by Jennifer Lindsay Knitwear Designs

Dotted Scarf

Judi Tepper based this scarf design on a stitch pattern she found in the book *Reversible Two-Color Knitting,* by Jane Neighbors (currently out of print). The contrast color is not knitted but rather woven back and forth into the main color knitted fabric. Made with cotton and silk, this scarf would be a great accessory for a denim jacket.

Finished Size
Width: 6½ inches (16.5 cm)
Length: 72 inches (182.5 cm) or desired length

Yarn
You will need about 475 yards (435 m) of medium-weight yarn in the same pattern and gauge, and about 125 yards (114 m) of medium-weight yarn in a contrast color for weaving. This yarn is worked with 2 strands held together.

We used Mission Falls 1824 Cotton (100% worsted-weight cotton; 84 yards [77 m]/ 1.75 ounce [50-g] ball):
#102 Ivory (main color), 475 yards (435 m)

Rowan Summer Tweed (70% silk, 30% cotton; 118 yards [108 m]/1.75-ounce [50-g] ball):
#509 Sunset (contrast color for weaving), 125 yards (114 m)
The contrast color is worked with 2 strands held together.

Needles
US size 9 (5.5 mm), double-point (dpn), set of 2, or a 16-inch (40-cm) long circular (circ), in order to slide stitches and work from other end of needle. ***Adjust the needle size if necessary to obtain the correct gauge.***

Gauge
16½ stitches and 25½ rows = 4 inches (10 cm) in pattern stitch

Notions
Tapestry needle

Special Abbreviations
Sl 1 wyib—slip 1 stitch with yarn held in back.
Sl 1 wyif—slip 1 stitch with yarn held in front.
Slip all stitches purlwise (pwise).

Note
For a more finished appearance along the edges, work a row of single crochet (see Techniques, page 114) around the outside edges of the scarf, at the same time working 3 single crochet in each corner stitch to smoothly round the corners and prevent puckering.

Woven Pattern Stitch
(worked over odd number of stitches)

Cast on (CO) with main color (MC) yarn.

Row 1: With MC, knit. Slide stitches (sts) to the other end of the needle.

Row 2: *(The* contrast color *[CC] yarn is woven between the stitches, and not knit.)* Holding 2 strands together, join CC, sl 1 wyib, *sl 1 wyif, sl 1 wyib*; repeat (rep) instructions between * * to end of row. Do not pull woven yarn too tightly or allow it to become too loose. Turn the work.

Rows 3–4: With MC, knit. Turn work.

Row 5: With CC, rep Row 2. Slide sts to other end of needle.

Row 6: With MC, knit. Turn work.

Row 7: With MC, knit. Slide sts to the other end of the needle.

Row 8: With CC, rep Row 2. Turn work.

Rep patt from Row 3, knitting two rows of MC and weaving 2 strands of CC across 1 row for patt.

Make the Scarf
With MC, loosely CO 27 sts. Work in Woven Patt St until scarf measures about 72 inches (182.5 cm) or desired length from CO edge. With MC, bind off (BO) all sts loosely.

Finishing
With a tapestry needle, weave in loose yarn tails along the side edges of work and secure.

Lacy Diamonds Scarf

Talented artist and knitting designer Linda Romens selected a beautiful color-blended yarn from LaLana Wools to use in this lacy panel scarf. Made with variegated medium-weight yarn, this design would look smashing worn with your favorite little black dress.

Finished Size
Width: 6 inches (15 cm)
Length: 60 inches (152.5 cm)

Yarn
You will need about 410 yards (375 m) total of medium-weight yarn

We used LaLana Wools Forever Random Blends (100% worsted-weight cotton; 82 yards [75 m]/2 ounce [57-g] skein):
Sonrisa, 5 skeins

Needles
US size 9 (5.5 mm). **Adjust the needle size if necessary to obtain the correct gauge.**

Gauge
12 stitches and 18 rows = 4 inches (10 cm) in pattern stitch

Notions
Tapestry needle

Pattern Stitch

Row 1 and all wrong side (WS) rows: K3, p13, k3.

Row 2: (right side [RS]) K7, knit 2 stitches together (k2tog), yarn over (yo), k1, yo, ssk, k7.

Row 4: K6, k2tog, yo, k3, yo, ssk, k6.

Row 6: K5, k2tog, yo, k5, yo, ssk, k5.

Row 8: K4, k2tog, yo, k1, k2tog, yo, k1, yo, ssk, k1, yo, ssk, k4.

Row 10: K3, k2tog, yo, k1, k2tog, yo, k3, yo, ssk, k1, yo, ssk, k3.

Row 12: K5, yo, ssk, k1, yo, slip (sl) 1, k2tog, pass slipped st over (psso), yo, k1, k2tog, yo, k5.

Row 14: K6, yo, ssk, k3, k2tog, yo, k6.

Row 16: K7, yo, ssk, k1, k2tog, yo, k7.

Row 18: K8, yo, sl 1, k2tog, psso, yo, k8.

Make the Scarf

Cast on (CO) 19 stitches (sts). Knit 4 rows (not shown on chart).

Next row: (WS) Follow chart or begin with Row 1 of text instructions for the pattern st. Repeat Rows 1–18 until the scarf measures about 1 inch (2.5 cm) from finished length, ending with Row 18. Work Row 1 once more. Knit 5 rows. Bind off.

Finishing

With tapestry needle, weave in loose yarn tails to WS of work and secure. Block the scarf, stretching the lace pattern to display the openwork.

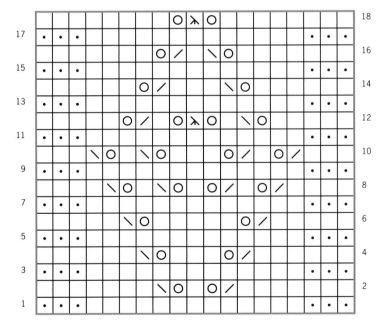

Key

□	Knit on RS, purl on WS
•	Purl on RS, knit on WS
＼	Ssk (see Abbreviations, page 120)
／	K2tog (see Abbreviations, page 120)
O	Yarn over
⋏	Sl 1, K2tog, psso (see Abbreviations, page 120)
□	Repeat pattern frame

Begin with Row 1 (WS of work), following chart from left to right.

Work Row 3 (RS of work), following chart from right to left.

Continue working chart through Row 18. Repeat Rows 1–18 until scarf measures about 1 inch (2.5 cm)

from finished length. Finish with Row 18, then work Row 1. Follow text instructions to finish.

Dashing Diagonal Scarf

Judi Tepper took two very different colorways and made a gorgeous scarf by using them in a simple diagonal pattern. Look through your stash and make a few small swatches of unlikely combinations. You might be pleasantly surprised with what you discover.

Finished Size
Width: 7 inches (18 cm)
Length: 60 inches (152.5 cm), not including fringe

Yarn
You will need about 420 yards (385 m) total in 2 colorways of medium-weight yarn, using the same stitch pattern and gauge. When adding fringe, cut the fringe strands first, before beginning the scarf, then work the scarf until you run out of yarn. Apply the fringe to each end after the scarf is finished.

We used Mountain Colors Mountain Goat (55% mohair, 45% wool: 240 yards [240 m]/4-ounce [114-g] skein):
Color A—Firestorm, 1 skein
Color B—Wilderness, 1 skein

Needles
US size 6 (4 mm) double-point (dpn) or 16-inch (40-cm) circular (circ). **Adjust the needle size if necessary to obtain the correct gauge.**

Gauge
18 stitches and 38 rows = 4 inches (10 cm) measured diagonally

Notions
US size H/8 (5 mm) or I/9 (5.5 mm) crochet hook to attach fringe to scarf ends; tapestry needle

Note
This scarf is made by working 2 rows of each color yarn and starting each color at the opposite ends of the needle. This will make one color dominant on one side and the other color dominant on the other side. Depending on which color you start with, that color will be the more dominant one, appearing along the "ridges," and the other color will be in the "valleys." This color effect is more noticeable when 2 solid colors are used. As you switch colors, make sure to wrap the yarns along the edge as you carry the yarn upward along the side.

Make the Scarf

Scarf Point, Increase Rows
With Color A, cast on (CO) 2 stitches (sts).

Row 1: With Color A, knit; slide sts to other end of the needle.

Row 2: With Color B, knit into the front and back loop of st (k1f&b), k1; turn work—(3 sts).

Row 3: With Color B, k1f&b, k2; slide sts to the other end of the needle—(4 sts).

Row 4: With Color A, k1f&b, knit to end; turn—(5 sts).

Row 5: With Color A, k1f&b, knit to end; slide sts to the other end of the needle—(6 sts).

Row 6: With Color B, k1f&b, knit to end; turn—(7 sts).

Row 7: With Color B, k1f&b, knit to end; slide sts to the other end of the needle—(8 sts).

Continue in this manner, knitting 2 rows of each color, and starting at opposite ends of the needle until there are about 50 sts on the needle or the desired width. The finished width of the scarf is measured along one straight edge of the triangle *opposite* the needle holding the sts and not along the sts on the needle.

Main Body—Diagonal Pattern
When the desired width is attained, and having completed two Color B rows, continue in the color pattern and the "slide and turn" method.

Row 1: With Color A, k1f&b on the first stitch in one row.

Row 2: With Color A, knit 2 stitches together (k2tog), knit to end; slide sts to the other end of the needle.

Row 3: With Color B, k2tog, knit to end; turn.

Row 4: With Color B, k1f&b, knit to end; slide sts to the other end of the needle.

As you continue, it will become obvious that you are increasing on the longer side and decreasing on the shorter side. When the longer side is almost as long as you want the scarf to be, begin the decrease rows.

Scarf Point, Decrease Rows
Continue in color patterning and the "slide and turn" method and k2tog at the beginning of each row until 1 st remains. Cut yarn, leaving a 4-inch (10-cm) tail. Insert the tail through the last st on the needle and pull to tighten.

Finishing

With a tapestry needle, weave in all yarn tails along the side edges and secure.

Fringe (optional)

Wind yarn around a 6-inch (15-cm) length of cardboard. Cut the yarn at one end to form 12-inch (31-cm) strands. Make 78 strands (39 on each scarf edge). *To make the fringe:*

Holding three strands of yarn together side by side, fold the strands in half to form a loop at one end. Working from front to back, insert the crochet hook into the first stitch on one end of the scarf. Catch the folded loops and pull through the work. Bring the cut ends through the folded loops and tighten; repeat instructions * * 13 times. Repeat fringe process on the other end of the scarf.

Techniques

Crochet and Knit

Crochet Chain

Even if you never plan to crochet a granny square, knowing the following crochet techniques will lend a polished look to your knitted treasures.

- Make a slipknot and place it on a crochet hook.

- *Bring the yarn over the hook as shown and draw it through the slipknot; repeat from * as many times as necessary.

- To finish off a crochet chain, cut the yarn and bring the yarn tail through the last loop on the crochet hook. Pull the yarn tail to tighten and secure.

Single Crochet

- Insert the hook into a stitch and bring the yarn over the hook from back to front and to the back again (a yarn over the hook); draw a loop through the stitch—(2 loops on hook).

- Yarn over the hook, and pull through both loops on the hook—(1 loop on hook).

- Move to the next stitch and repeat instructions from beginning.

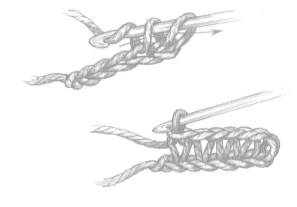

Provisional (Temporary) Crochet Chain Cast-on

● With crochet hook and waste yarn, make a crochet chain (see Crochet Chain) using a few more stitches than specified for the cast-on number. Cut the yarn, leaving a 4-inch (10-cm) tail; thread the tail through the last loop on the hook; and pull to secure.

● Tie a knot in the waste yarn tail to help you identify this end later, when it's time to remove the chain.

● The crochet chain has a smooth side with Vs and the other side has a bump in the center of each V. The side with the bumps is the one you want to use for the next step.

● Work the first Row (Round): Beginning at the opposite end of the waste yarn knot, join the main yarn. *Insert knitting needle under the first crochet bump, wrap the yarn around the needle as if to knit, and pull up a loop—(1 stitch on needle); repeat from * for the desired number of stitches.

Removing a Provisional Cast-On

● To remove the provisional cast-on, pull out end of the waste yarn from the last crochet stitch and then carefully pull the waste yarn to remove the provisional cast-on and release the live stitches. Insert a knitting needle into the live stitches to seat them on the needle.

Seamless Beginning
This technique can be used to start socks, mittens, and hats.

● After picking up the required number of stitches from a provisional cast-on with a double-point needle, knit the designated number of rows (in the case of our illustration, 4 rows). Remove the provisional cast-on and insert a double-pointed needle into the live stitches. One double-point needle holds stitches at one end and a second double-point needle holds an equal number of stitches on the other end.

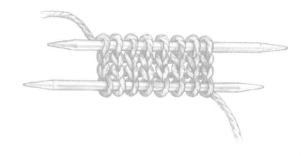

Embroidery Stitches

Lazy Daisy Stitch

The lazy daisy stitch is often used to make flower petals or a chain. The petals are formed in a ring with the base of each petal positioned close to the others. When several petal stitches are worked in a line, a chain is formed.

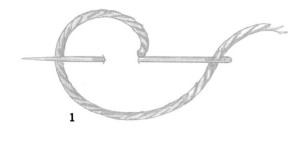

- Bring the threaded needle to the front of the fabric where the petal base should begin. Reinsert the needle into the fabric, a thread or two away from where you started, but do not draw the thread all the way through.

- *Bring the needle back up through the fabric at the spot designated for the top of the petal, or chain, *at the same time* looping the yarn counterclockwise and passing under the needle. To repeat the process when making a petal, reinsert the needle on the other side of the looped

thread to anchor the petal in place. Take needle and thread to wrong side and move the needle to the left or right of the first petal base to make the next stitch. Repeat from * until petals form a ring.

Embroidered Chain Stitch

The chain stitch is an uninterrupted row of lazy daisy petals. If making a chain, work the first step of lazy daisy stitch. Then proceed as follows.

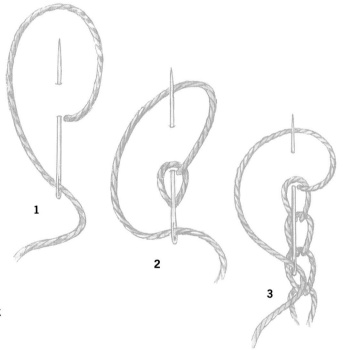

- *Bring the needle back up through the fabric at the spot designated for the top of the chain, *at the same time* looping the yarn counterclockwise and passing under the needle.

- Reinsert the needle to back of fabric at the top of the chain, about a half stitch over from the point where the needle came out in step 1.

- Keeping each chain stitch the same size, repeat from * in step 1 until chain is desired length. To end the chain, insert the needle into the fabric just over the looped yarn, take it to the back of the fabric, and secure.

Vertical Duplicate Stitch
Like its name, duplicate stitch replicates the knit stitch. This technique completely covers the knitted stitch beneath and is a great way to add small sections of color; the technique can also be used to hide mistakes in your work.

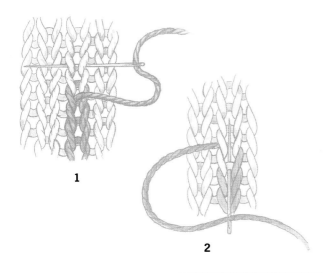

1

2

- Thread needle with about 18 inches (46 cm) of yarn (rethread as necessary). Longer yarn lengths will fray and lose fibers as you pull the yarn through the stitches.

- Begin the first stitch by starting at the lowest point of the design or stitches to be covered. Secure the yarn on the wrong side of the fabric.

- Bring the needle to the fabric front at the base of the first stitch. *Insert the needle at the top of the same stitch, from right to left. Pull yarn to front of fabric, then reinsert needle at base.

- For the next stitch, working one row above, bring the needle out to the front through the center of the stitch above the first duplicate stitch, and repeat from * as desired.

French Knot
French knots are frequently used in embroidery and in knitting to add small raised dots.

- Bring a threaded tapestry needle to the right side of the work at the position where you want the knot. Grasp the yarn between your left thumb and index finger about 1 inch (2.5 cm) away from the surface of the fabric and hold the strand so it is taut.

- With your left hand, wrap the strand of yarn one or more times around the needle. (More wraps make a more prominent knot.)

- Holding the yarn taut again, insert the point of the needle into the knitted material about 1 or 2 threads from the starting point. Take it to the wrong side of the fabric, *at the same time* holding the yarn down with a thumb. Release your thumb as you carefully pull the thread through to the wrong side to set the knot.

1

2

3

Seams

Note: When seaming, always leave a beginning and ending yarn tail of at least 4 inches (10 cm) to weave to the wrong side of work and secure after the seam is finished.

Backstitch
This seaming technique, which produces a firm, stable seam, is used on both horizontal and vertical seams.

- With threaded tapestry needle and right sides of work together, insert needle through both layers of fabric from front to back. Bring needle out to front side again about 1 or 2 stitches to the left of entry point. Pull yarn through to front.

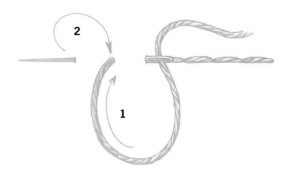

- Moving back and to the right of entry point by one stitch, reinsert needle to back. Moving forward again, to the left, bring the needle out to the front of work, about one or two stitches ahead of the first sewing stitch.

- Repeat as necessary to close the fabric pieces together.

Mattress Stitch
This method is often called an invisible seam. When worked correctly, it has a seamless appearance.

- With threaded tapestry needle, right sides of work facing upward, and both pieces lying on a flat surface, *insert the needle tip under the horizontal strand between the first and second stitches of one fabric piece.

- Move across to the adjacent fabric piece and insert the needle under the horizontal strand between the first and second stitches. Gently pull yarn to tighten*.

- Moving up one or two rows, repeat instructions from * to * until seam is finished and the fabric pieces are joined.

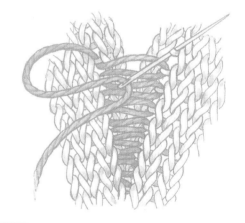

Whipstitch

- Place both fabric pieces to be joined with right sides together.

- *With threaded needle, insert needle through the edge stitch on one piece and through the corresponding edge stitch on the adjacent piece. Pull yarn or thread through. Keep sewing yarn at same tension as knitting. Don't pull too tightly, or the seam will pucker.

- Move to next stitch and repeat process from *.

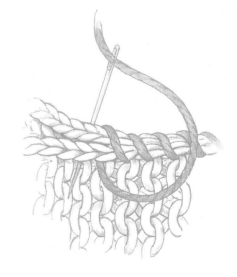

Finishing

Decrease Bind-Off

Method 1: Knit 2 together, *slip remaining stitch back to left needle, knit 2 together; repeat from * to end of row.

Method 2: Knit 2 together through back loops, *slip remaining stitch back to left needle, knit 2 together through back loops; repeat from * to end of row.

Hiding Yarn Tails Along Side Seams

One of the easiest places to hide loose yarn tails is in the side seam. This is not always possible when knitting in the round or when working intarsia. When joining the yarns at the side seam, simply start knitting with a new yarn, leaving a 4-inch (10-cm) tail of each strand. Make a temporary knot to hold the old and new yarns together, especially if the yarns are slippery.

● Untie the temporary knot if there is one.

● Thread one strand of the loose yarn through a tapestry needle and weave it in and out of the side edge stitches, working upward. Thread the second yarn tail through a tapestry needle and work the same as before, but moving downward this time. Trim the ends even with the knitting.

● Yarn tails that are too short to thread through a tapestry needle can be maneuvered with the help of a crochet hook. Insert the hook under a stitch, latch onto the short tail, and pull it through the stitch. Repeat as many times as possible.

● When a yarn is very slippery, such as ribbon, weave the yarn tail through the stitches as usual, but leave about ½-inch (1.3-cm) at the end. With matching sewing thread and needle, tack down the remaining end securely, making sure the sewing stitches aren't visible on the right side of the fabric.

Hiding Ends in the Middle of Your Work

When it's necessary to join yarn in the middle of the work (as when working intarsia or Fair Isle), it's best to weave the yarn horizontally or diagonally through the stitches on the wrong side of the work. When finishing old yarns and joining new ones, always leave at least 4-inch (10-cm) tails to ensure adequate length to weave in and secure.

On the purl side of stockinette stitch, the purl stitches are formed by upper and lower bumps. Weave the yarn tails as follows:

● Working with the yarn tail on your right and using a tapestry needle, weave the yarn in and out of the lower bumps to the left of where the two yarns meet.

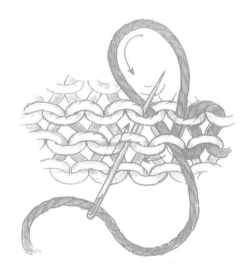

● Working with the yarn tail on your left, weave the yarn in and out of the lower bumps to the right of where the two yarns meet.

Abbreviations

beg—begin; beginning; begins

bet—between

BO—bind off; binding off; bound off

CC—contrast color(s)

ch—chain, as in crochet

cm—centimeters

CO—cast on; casting on

cont—continue; continuing; continued

dec(s)—decrease(s); decreasing; decreased

dpn—double-point needles

foll—follow; following

fwd—forward

g—gram(s)

inc—increase(s); increasing; increased

k—knit

k1f&b—knit into the front and then the back loop of the same stitch

k2tog—knit two stitches together

kwise—knitwise (as if to knit)

m—marker

m1—make one stitch (increase) —insert the left needle from back to front under the horizontal strand between the stitch on the left needle and the one just worked, forming a loop on the left needle; then, with the right needle, knit into the front strand of the loop, thereby twisting the stitch and closing any hole.

MC—main color

mm—millimeter(s)

p—purl

p1f&b—purl into front and then the back loop of the same stitch

p2tog—purl two stitches together

patt(s)—pattern(s)

pm—place marker

psso—pass slipped stitch over

pwise—purlwise (as if to purl)

rem—remain; remaining; remainder

rep—repeat(s); repeating; repeated

rev sc—reverse single crochet, also known as crab stitch

rev St st—reverse Stockinette stitch (the purl side of St st is used as the right side)

rib—ribbing

rnd(s)—round(s), as in circular knitting

RS—right side

sc—single crochet

sk—skip

sl—slip

sl st—slip stitch

ssk—slip two stitches knitwise, one at a time, from the left needle to the right needle. Insert the left needle tip into the fronts of both slipped stitches and knit them together from this position.

st(s)—stitch(es)

St st—stockinette stitch

tbl—through the back loop of a stitch

tog—together

WS—wrong side

wyib—with the yarn in back of the work

wyif—with the yarn in front of the work

yo—yarn over

*—repeat starting point (i.e., repeat from *)

* *—repeat all instructions between asterisks

( ) alternate measurements and/or instructions

[ ] instructions worked as a group for a specified number of times

Resources

Yarn Companies

Artful Yarns/JCA, Inc.
35 Scales Lane
Townsend, MA 01469–1094
Tel: 978–597–8794

Catnip Friends, page 88

Berroco
P.O. Box 367
14 Elmdale Road
Uxbridge, MA 01569
Tel: 508–278–2527

Disco Purse, page 28

Black Water Abbey
P.O. Box 470688
Aurora, CO 80047–0688
Tel: 702–320–1003
E-mail: marilyn@abbeyyarns.com
www.abbeyyarns.com

*Pampered Pooch Striped Sweater,
page 91*

Blue Heron
29532 Canvasback Drive #6
Easton, MD 21601
Tel: 410–819–0401
E-mail:blueheronyarns
@verizon.net
www.blueheronyarns.com

Small Shawl, page 32

Blue Sky Alpacas, Inc.
P.O. Box 387
St. Francis, MN 55070
Tel: 763–753–5815
Fax: 763–753–3345
E-mail: bluesky@visi.com
www.blueskyalpacas.com

*Buttons and Stripes Ribbed Scarf,
page 103*

Brooks Farm Fiber
412 Old Red Oak Road
Lancaster, TX 75146
Tel: 972–227–1593
E-mail: bfarm@att.net

*Easy Side-to-Side Garter Scarf,
page 100*

Brown Sheep Yarn Co.
100662 County Road
Mitchell, NE 69357–9748
Tel: 308–635–2198
Order line: 800–826–9136
Fax: 308–635–2143
www.brownsheep.com

*Amish-Inspired Afghan,
page 76*

Classic Elite
300 Jackson Street
Lowell, MA 01852
Tel: 978–453–2837
Order line: 800–343–0308
Fax: 978–452–3058
E-mail: classicelite@aol.com

*I-80 Poncho, page 44; Kerchief, page
32; Medium Shawl, page 32; San
Francisco Headbands, page 50;
Trellis Pillow, page 70*

Colinette
(U.S.A.)
Unique Kolours
1428 Oak Lane
Downingtown, PA 19335
Tel: 610–280–7720
Fax: 610–280–7701
E-mail: uniquekolo@aol.com
www.uniquekolours.com

(Great Britain)
Banwy Workshop
Llanfair Caereinion
Powys, Mid Wales SY210SG
Tel: 011–44–1938–810128
Fax: 011–44–1938–810127

Diagonal Scarves, page 38

Color Me . . . Yarn Co.
161 County Road 441
Thorndale, TX 76577
Tel: 877–783–1310
Fax: 512–898–5113
www.colormeyarn.com

Diagonal Scarves, page 38

Crystal Palace
160 23rd Street
Richmond, CA 94804
Tel: 510–237–9988
www.straw.com

San Francisco Headbands, page 50

Dale of Norway, Inc.
N16 W23390 Stonebridge Drive
Suite A
Waukesha, WI 53188
Tel: 262–544–1996
Fax: 262–544–1997
www.dale.no

*San Francisco Headbands, page 50;
Easy Rolled-Edge Hat, page 55*

**Filatura Di Crosa
Tahki/Stacy Charles, Inc./
Filatura di Crosa**
8000 Cooper Avenue, Bldg. 1
Glendale, NY 11385
www.tahkistacycharles.com

*Fiesta Bag, page 30; San Francisco
Headbands, page 50*

Harrisville Designs
Center Village
P.O. Box 806
Harrisville, NH 03450
Tel: 603–827–3333
Order line: 800–338–9415
Fax: 603–827–3335
www.harrisville.com

Mini Christmas Stockings, page 67

Jaeger Handknits USA
Westminster Fibers
dba Jaeger Handknits USA
4 Townsend West #8
Nashua, NH 03063
Tel: 603–886–5041
Fax: 603–886–1056
E-mail:
info@westminsterfibers.com
www.knitrowan.com

*Classic Rugby Stripe Scarf,
page 107*

Jager Farm Icelandics
75 Mountain Street
Haydenville, MA 01039
Tel: 413–268–3086
www.jager-icelandics.com

Lavender Sachet, page 15

LaLana Wools
136 Paseo Norte
Taos, NM 87571
Tel: 505–758–9631
Order line: 888–377–9631
E-mail: lalana@lalanawools.com
www.lalanawools.com

*Amulet Pouch, page 26;
Walk on the Wild Side Slipper Socks,
page 57; Lacy Diamonds Scarf,
page 110*

Lion Brand
34 West 15th Street
New York, NY 10011
Tel: 800–795–LION
www.lionbrand.com

Knitted Kick Sacks, page 83

Mini-Mills Ltd.
RR#1
Belfast
Prince Edward Island
Canada C0A1A0
Tel/Fax: 902–659–2248
Order line: 800–827–3397
www.minimills.net

Sumptuously Soft Scarf, page 96

Mission Falls
(U.S.A.)
Unique Kolours
1428 Oak Lane
Downingtown, PA 19335
Tel: 610–280–7720
Fax: 610–280–7701
E-mail: uniquekolo@aol.com
www.uniquekolours.com

(Great Britain)
Banwy Workshop
Llanfair Caereinion
Powys, Mid Wales SY210SG
Tel: 011–44–1938–810128
Fax: 011–44–1938–810127

*Ted's Scarf, page 42; Dotted Scarf,
page 108*

Mostly Merino
P.O. Box 878
Putney, VT 05346
Tel: 802–254–7436
merino@together.net

*Easy Side-to-Side Garter Scarf,
page 100*

Mountain Colors
P.O. Box 156
Corvallis, MT 59870
Tel: 406–777–2277

Dashing Diagonal Scarf, page 112

Nature's Palette
Darlene Hayes
Hand Jive Knits
Tel: 916–806–8063
E-mail: darlenehayes@hand-
jiveknits.com
www.handjiveknits.com

*Ruffled Baby Tube Socks, Mitts, and
Caps, page 84; Herringbone Scarf
with Moorish Tassels, page 104*

On Line
Knitting Fever, Inc., and
Euro Yarns
35 Debevoise Avenue
Roosevelt, NY 11575
Tel: 516–546–3600
Fax: 516–546–6871

*San Francisco Headbands,
page 50*

Raumagarn Finull Garn
Nordic Fiber Arts
4 Cutts Road
Durham, NH 03824
Tel: 603–868–1196
www.nordicfiberarts.com

Easy Rolled-Edge Hat, page 55

Reynolds/JCA, Inc.
35 Scales Lane
Townsend, MA 01469–1094
Tel: 978–597–8794

*Felted Patchwork Rug,
page 74*

Rowan
Westminster Fibers
dba Rowan USA
4 Townsend West #8
Nashua, NH 03063
Tel: 603–886–5041
Fax: 603–886–1056
E-mail:
info@westminsterfibers.com
www.knitrowan.com

*Easy Rolled-Edge Hat, page 55;
Curlilocks Finger Puppet, page 80;
Catnip Friends, page 88; Dotted
Scarf, page 108*

Treenway Silks
501 Musgrove Road
Salt Spring Island
British Columbia
Canada V8K 1V5
Tel: 888–383–7455
E-mail: silk@treenwaysilks.com
www.treenwaysilks.com

*Silk Bamboo Ribbed Scarf,
page 99*

Trendsetter
16742 Stagg #104
Van Nuys, CA 91406
Tel: 818–780–5497
Order line: 800–446–2425
E-mail: trndstr@aol.com

*Disco Purse, page 28; Fiesta Bag,
page 30*

Weaving Southwest
216-B Paseo del Pueblo Norte
Taos, NM 87571
Tel: 505–758–0433
Fax: 505–758–5839
E-mail: weaving@weavingsouth-west.com
www.weavingsouthwest.com

Skullcaps, pages 61, 62

Beads, Buttons, Charms, Fabrics

Banksville Designer Fabrics
115 New Canaan Avenue
(Route 123)
Norwalk, CT 06850
Tel: 203–846–1333

Beadworks
139 Washington Street
Norwalk, CT 06854
Tel: 203–852–9194
www.beadworks.com

Blue Santa Beads
17 Northgate Village
Media, PA 19063
Tel: 610–892–2847
E-mail: bluesantabeads@aol.com

Big Eye needles

Dwellings Revisited
10 Bent Street
P.O. Box 470
Taos, NM 87571
Tel: 505–758–3377

Skull beads, other beads, charms, and trinkets

Main Street Bead Studio
502 North Main Street
Fremont, NE 68025
Tel: 402–721–9656

Thunder Lizard
1803 Highway 68
P.O. Box 1089
Ranchos de Taos, NM 87557
Tel: 505–751–1752
Fax: 505–751–1901

Beads, charms, trinkets

Tin-Nee-Ann Trading Co.
923 Cerrillos Road
Santa Fe, NM 87505
Tel: 505–988–1630
Fax: 505–988–2938
Order line: 800–255–5491

Beads, charms, trinkets

Lavender

Cynthia Alexander
P.O. Box 7501
Wilton, CT 06897
www.cynthia-alexander.com
Tel: 203–834–2507
Fax: 203–834–1319

Knitting and Spinning Supplies

Woodland Woolworks
P.O. Box 850
Carlton, OR 97111
Tel: 503–852–7376
Order line: 800–547–3725
Fax: 503–852–6685
E-mail: info@woolworks.com
www.woolworks.com

Leather soles

The WoolRoom
172 Joe's Hill Road
Brewster, NY 10507
Tel: 845-279-7627
Fax: 845-278-5947
E-mail: susan@woolroom.com
www.woolroom.com

McMorran scale

Charities for Yarn Contributions

Visit www.interweave.com/knit/charities.asp for an extensive list of charities.

Author's Web site

www.cooknit.com

Index

Project Index

This illustrated guide is organized by yarn weight, so you can quickly locate a suitable project for your stash.

Super Fine
1 Curlilocks Finger Puppet, page 80
2 Lavender Sachet, page 15

Fine
3 Amulet Pouch, page 26
4 Striped Skullcap, page 61
5 Checkered Skullcap, page 62
6 Ruffled Baby Tube Socks, Mitts, and Caps, page 84
7 Buttons and Stripes Ribbed Scarf, 103
8 Herringbone Scarf with Moorish Tassels, page 104
9 Classic Rugby Stripe Scarf, page 107

Light
10 Trellis Pillow, page 70
11 Sumptuously Soft Scarf, page 96

Medium
12 Knitted Kick Sacks, page 83
13 Catnip Friends, page 88
14 Mini Christmas Stockings, page 67
15 San Francisco Headbands, page 50
16 Triple Triangle Extravaganza, page 32
17 Walk on the Wild Side Slipper Socks, page 57
18 Pampered Pooch Striped Sweater, page 91
19 Ted's Scarf, page 42

Yarn Index

The yarn amounts listed here reflect the approximate number of yards (meters) in the project. Turn to the project page to find how these amounts may be divided into more than one color or yarn type.

YARN WEIGHT	TOTAL # YARDS (M)	PROJECT	PAGE
Super Fine	1–3 yards (91.5 –275 cm)	Finger Puppet	80
Super Fine	37 yards (34 m)	Lavender Sachet	15
Fine	14–15 yards (13–14 m)	Amulet Pouch	26
Fine	175 yards (160 m)	Skullcaps	61, 62
Fine	185 yards (169 m)	Baby Set	84
Light	544 yards (497 m)	Trellis Pillow	70
Medium	10 yards (9 m)	Knitted Kick Sacks	83
Medium	23 yards (21 m)	Catnip Friends	88
Medium	30 yards (28 m)	Mini Stockings	67
Medium	52 yards (47.5 m)	Headbands	50
Medium	95 yards (87 m)	Kerchief	32
Medium	150 yards (137 m)	Slipper Socks	57
Medium-Ribbon	158 yards (144 m)	Ribbon Scarf	38
Medium-Mohair	200 yards (183 m)	Mohair Scarf	38
Medium	274 yards (250 m)	Pampered Pooch	91
Medium	460 yards (420 m)	Small Shawl	32
Medium	518 yards (473 m)	Medium Shawl	32
Medium	680 yards (622 m)	Ted's Scarf	42
Medium	1883 yards (1722 m)	I-80 Poncho	44
Medium	1970 yards (1801 m)	Amish Afghan	76
Medium	60 yards (56 m)	Disco Purse	28
Novelty	10 yards (9 m)	Fiesta Bag	30
Bulky	810 yards (740 m)	Patchwork Rug	74
Super Bulky	66 yards (60 m)	Rolled-Edge Hat	55

SPECIAL SCARF SECTION

YARN WEIGHT	TOTAL # YARDS (M)	PROJECT	PAGE
Fine	480 yards (439 m)	Buttons and Stripes	103
Fine	500 yards (457 m)	Herringbone	104
Fine	525 yards (480 m)	Classic Rugby	107
Light	275 yards (251 m)	Sumptuously Soft	96
Medium	300 yards (274 m)	Silk Bamboo	99
Medium	325 yards (297 m)	Side-to-Side	100
Medium	410 yards (375 m)	Lacy Diamonds	110
Medium	420 yards (384 m)	Dashing Diagonal	112
Medium	600 yards (549 m)	Dotted Scarf	108